Praise for A Journey of Awakening

"Rabbi Ted Falcon has a blessed gift for illuminating a clear and progressive path of contemplative practice that brings the Mystery—in all its many dimensions—more fully alive in our daily lives.

"Taken to heart, these meditations will awaken in you a profound sense of awe, wonder, and realization of many new dimensions of spiritual insight.

"In this gem of a book, Rabbi Ted offers us a long-awaited lamp of wisdom illuminating an inner journey of a lifetime. The reader is invited onto this path of awakening with clarity, warmth, and accessibility, by an inspired and trustworthy guide and companion who knows the way from the inside out. A real treasure!"

Joel Levey, Ph.D., and Michelle Levey, M.A., authors of *Living in Balance*; *A Simple Guide to Meditation and Relaxation*; **and** *Wisdom at Work*

"Rabbi Falcon's meditations guide us as we traverse each year's wilderness. Experiencing the beauty and awareness this brings us as a couple has enriched our lives immensely."

Linda & Gerry Owen, Marriage & Family Therapists

"Each year, these Kabbalistic meditations guide me to a deepening revelation of my own uniqueness."

Deloris Tarzan Ament, Author, *Iridescent Light: The Emergence of Northwest Art*

A
Journey
of
Awakening

Kabbalistic Meditations on the Tree of Life

Rabbi Ted Falcon, Ph.D.

Skynear Press

Cover design by David Blatner, moo.com, and David Marty Design

This is a significantly revised edition of
A Journey of Awakening:
49 Steps from Enslavement to Freedom
© 1999 Theodore G. Falcon

Printed in the United States of America

Library of Congress Cataloging-in-Publication Data
Falcon, Theodore G., 1942–
A Journey of Awakening: Kabbalistic Meditations on
the Tree of Life / Ted Falcon
          p.   cm.
ISBN 0-9670547-0-2
LCCN 2003103507

Spiritual life—Judaism. 2. Self-actualization (Psychology)—
Religious aspects—Judaism. 3. Sefirot (Cabala) I. Title

Published by Skynear Press
P.O. Box 51241
Seattle, WA 98115-1241
skynear@innerfaith.org

Dedication

To Ruth Ann Neuwald Falcon with deep love and gratitude, and to all my students and friends who have put up with me over these years, and from whom I have learned more than I ever could have imagined.

In Memory

Natalie R. Falcon
1914–2001

CONTENTS

Acknowledgments

Ever since the first rendering of these meditations appeared on a computer bulletin board system in Los Angeles in 1986, they have been enriched by many who utilized them in their spiritual process. I am grateful to all who have encouraged me over the years to prepare them for publication.

Makom Ohr Shalom, a synagogue for Jewish meditation and spirituality in Los Angeles, was the context in which so much of my teaching unfolded. Bet Alef Meditative Synagogue in Seattle, where the teaching has matured, provides a deep and loving environment for the expansion of Jewish spirituality. My life has been incredibly enriched by those in Los Angeles and in Seattle who have shared this journey with me.

My wife, Ruth, loved me even through some surprisingly stressful times during our journey with this manuscript. In so very many ways she has supported me in my work, and has taken responsibility for editing, coordination, and organization that seem beyond me in this life. There have been many times when she was able to keep me on track when I had lost my way.

During the production of the first edition, David Blatner was the angel who designed the original cover and held my hand through the various and mostly predictable computer emergencies. His example reminded me that Beginner's Mind is a benefit in meditation, but not in computer program management. As this significant revision of the original text goes to press, I owe special gratitude to Ruth's editing skills, to Sheryn Hara, of Hara Publishing Group, for coordinating this project, and to Stephanie Martindale, for her creative lay-out skills.

The spiritual journey reflected in these pages is a journey of a lifetime. Although there is within us a self who wants immediate enlightenment, that is rarely the way of true growth.

One of my early teachers, Ken Keyes, Jr., wrote that spiritual awakening could take as long as five years of serious practice. He taught me that over 25 years ago, and I am not there yet. But the meditations and the kabbalistic insights which you will meet in this book have deeply enhanced my journey, as I hope they will support yours.

When the first printing of this book sold out, I received many requests for a second printing. The changes in this edition benefit from comments from those who have used that book as a support for their meditative journey. I am grateful for that feedback, and invite your responses, as well.

May these pages help you to better know your Path, that your actions in the world might flow from greater Wisdom and Compassion. And on your journey, may you always go from strength to Strength, from love to Love, and from life to Life.

Ted Falcon
Seattle, 2003
rabbi@innerfaith.org

שִׁוִּיתִי יהוה לְנֶגְדִּי תָמִיד:

Shiviti Adonai l'negdi tamid.

I set the Eternal (*Yod–Hay–Vav–Hay*) before me always.

Psalm 16:8

Introduction

The universal hallmark of mystical experience—the Realization of Connection, Wholeness, and Oneness—carries the conviction of such unparalleled Truth that its sharing becomes a highest priority. While itself beyond words, every spiritual tradition contains extensive writings attempting to convey the significance of this Realization.

The Realization, however, always opens from the inside out and, in the very telling, we tend to gradually replace the actual lived Realization with the story we tell about it. We tend to talk about that Moment but actually avoid the lived Moment in Itself.

Through a series of contemplations and meditations, this book invites you to move beyond words that you might taste what mystics through the ages have attempted to convey. It provides you with support for the deeper exploration of your own journey of awareness, as you become more familiar with some of the key concepts of the Jewish mystical tradition while engaging in your inner explorations. The meditations invite you to engage directly in the Awakening that is your birthright. To maximize your ability to appreciate your own development, keeping a meditative journal is encouraged.

One of the clearest and most enduring paradigms of spiritual awakening in the Jewish mystical tradition is represented by the ancient journey from the enslavement in Egypt to the awakening of Revelation at Sinai. The steps in this process are reflected in the 49 days between Passover and *Shavuot*, the Feast of Weeks, which commemorates the receiving of the Ten Commandments while standing at Sinai.

The word "Egypt" in Hebrew is *Mitzrayim*, signifying "tight places," or "places of contraction and stuckness." Internally, this stuckness refers to times in which we are caught in our lesser identities and are, indeed, limited by our contracted consciousness. From that place we are not available to hear the greater teaching.

This metaphor describes a journey in which all spiritual seekers engage. Many have noted that it is far simpler to get the person out of Egypt than it is to get the Egypt out of the person. While we might at first imagine that we are enslaved by others, and by events in the outer world, during the early stages of a spiritual process it becomes increasingly clear that the responsibility for our experience and our evolution is our own.

The meditations in this book follow the 49-day paradigm developed in the Kabbalah based on that ancient biblical journey. At Sinai, we are available for what we cannot hear from the places of our stuckness. At Sinai, we open ourselves to the deeper truths of our own beings, and to the deeper Reality of the One Being we share.

In this text you will find meditative readings and intentions for each of the seven weeks of this process, followed by daily meditations adding the unique energies of each day. Weekly and daily focus phrases provide steps along a meditative path toward self-awakening.

No matter what your previous experience with meditation or with spiritual process, this book is designed to support your growing. If you like, you can turn to any page in the text and begin there. Or you may use the introduction to the framework of the Kabbalistic Tree of Life to help you further understand how the meditative focus for each day emerges, and to guide you on your own journey to that place of hearing.

Here, then, is a handbook to support the unfolding of the greater Awareness that yearns to awaken more fully through you.

Beginning this Journey of Awakening

An intention, in Hebrew, a *kavvanah*, provides a channel through which energy can flow. Our goals and purposes in life, when made specific, serve as beacons toward which we move, and provide criteria with which to determine how far we have come and how far we have yet to go. Without clear intentions, our energy tends to be fragmented, and our personal evolution is slowed. Awareness of our individual intentions can begin the process of choosing more significant intentions for our relationships, our families, our communities, and our world.

The most helpful intentions follow from an understanding of the fuller nature of our current experience in the world as well as from the direction in which we choose to travel. While you can turn immediately to the meditations in this book, the following information will provide grounding for a more fruitful experience.

The Basic Shape of this Meditative Process

The meditations in this text are based on the energies of the kabbalistic Tree of Life. This "tree" is made up of ten *sefirot*, or levels, reflecting the ways reality unfolds from the least manifest state of being to become the world we know. We begin with an introduction to these ten levels. Then we focus on the lower seven *sefirot* as they are utilized for the 49-day process of spiritual expansion called the *Counting of the Omer*.

In Jewish tradition, the *Omer* period marks the literal 49 days between the festivals of Passover and *Shavuot* in the spring of each year. Passover, called *Pesach* in Hebrew, presents images of an ancient Exodus when the Hebrew People made their way from enslavement toward freedom, and represents the ever-present challenge of stepping out from personal places of stuckness and limitation toward greater awareness and responsibility. The festival of *Shavuot* (literally, "Weeks") occurs seven weeks later, when our People stood to receive Torah at the mountain of Revelation called Sinai.

This seven-week period probably first existed to honor an agricultural rhythm beginning with the spring barley harvest and concluding with the later harvest of wheat. The Bible indicates that on the *Shabbat* following Passover (interpreted by the early rabbis to mean the second day of Passover), a sheaf of barley (in Hebrew, an *omer*) is waved, and then 49 days that lead to the later harvest are counted.

As time went on, these days of *Omer* counting became related to the historical journey of our ancestors from enslavement toward freedom. Later, during the mystical expansion of the sixteenth century, these 49 days were recognized as a paradigm for personal renewal and spiritual awakening. The tight or stuck places for which *Mitzrayim* (Egypt) is a metaphor exist within the self, to be discovered and released as we grow. Spiritual awakening requires releasing ourselves from our inner enslavements to old patterns, old self-definitions, old beliefs.

At the end of the series of 49 meditative readings and focus phrases, there are meditations of culmination. When used during the actual *Omer* period, they occur on *Shavuot*. Whenever in the year you reach them, these concluding meditations help complete a process of opening more fully and grounding your awakening that you might better translate your spiritual awareness into more compassionate action in the world.

Meditation

This is a book of meditative possibilities, an invitation to deepen your awareness of the nature of your being. Meditation is a path toward that which is Universal in human experience. And while that Universal awareness transcends any particular religious or spiritual path, an authentic path is tremendously supportive of the journey.

In Jewish tradition, as in all authentic spiritual paths, meditation forms a strong foundation supporting the journey to more spiritual awareness. It has often been said that prayer involves *talking* to God (whatever one's conception of that Being), and meditation involves *listening* to God. Meditation provides an avenue through which we become available for a more inclusive awareness of our relationship to ourselves, to each other, and to our world.

Some meditative techniques, such as those that focus on the breath itself, or on the continual flow of awareness in the conscious mind, are shared by many traditions. The two Hebrew words that are used to mean "meditation" each express a particular path. *Hitbon'nut*, best translated "contemplation," literally means "self-understanding." *Hitbod'dut*, usually translated "meditation," literally means "being alone with oneself."

Jewish meditation springs from the culture, traditions, texts, and rituals of Judaism. Where Hindu meditations might focus on a word in the Sanskrit language, Hebrew, as well as Jewish images, language, yearly cycle, history, and symbols provide the grounding for Jewish meditation.

Specific meditative techniques help us direct our attention rather than simply allowing our minds to run away with us. As we focus, the mind tends to relax a little, and we slow down enough to hear its restless thought-creations. As we develop the capacity to witness this creation without judgment, and without getting caught up in any particular image or story, we begin to appreciate that we are far more than the functioning of our minds. We *have* thoughts, but we are not our thoughts. We *have* stories, but we are not our stories.

Through meditation, a more inclusive identity begins to awaken. These fruits of meditation flower on the other side of words. Meditation opens us to dimensions of knowing always greater than the words that attempt to describe them.

Spirituality

Spirituality is a word often used to refer to meaningful experiences, or to that which is considered especially good or valuable. Many use the word to direct our attention to that which is deeper within ourselves—to a greater Self, to a greater Wisdom, to a greater Love. I prefer to use *spiritual* to refer specifically to the Realization of Unity. This is an operational kind of definition, in which spirituality relates to the degree to which we are conscious of the interconnectedness of all being.

The less spiritual our awareness, the more we perceive separation and fragmentation. Our degree of spiritual perception is directly related to the extent to which we feel a sense of belonging—of being in the right place, at the right time, doing the right thing. Our lack of spiritual consciousness is measured by the degree of alienation and confusion we experience. The more spiritual the identity, the more inclusive it is; the less spiritual the identity, the more exclusive. Spirituality, in this sense, relates to perception, understanding, and experience—it is more a matter of *being* than a way of thinking.

On the mental level, spirituality reflects itself as a greater clarity and connection to deep inner resources of Wisdom and

Knowing. We are able to know ourselves as participants in a Universal Life. On an emotional level, spirituality expresses in the enhanced capacity to experience and share love and compassion. On a physical level, spirituality manifests in a sense of harmony, balance, and rightness. Spirituality expressing on emotional and physical levels does not require perfectly smooth relationships or perfect physical health. It requires greater acceptance and the release of resistance, so that the radical fullness of each moment might be met. (non-striving)

Spiritualized consciousness opens us to the healing nature of Awareness itself. With an expanding awareness, there is a greater ability to appreciate the unique beings we are and to perceive the special gifts we each carry. With a greater ability to know Oneness, we understand more fully the truths of spiritual teachings from all traditions. A greater possibility of individual and of world healing naturally begins to manifest.

This book provides clear and direct avenues that you can travel as you move toward greater spiritual awakening. These paths are constructed of meditative practices and kabbalistic insights designed to encourage the expansion of your own inner wisdom. Spiritual consciousness is the fullest freedom, as we become more able to participate in the great work called *tikkun olam*—the realization of deep Peace and Wholeness to which we are each called.

Kabbalah

Many aspects of Jewish mysticism and spiritual teaching are referred to as the "*kabbalah*," the literal meaning of which is "that which is received." The Kabbalah contains evolving expressions and understandings of revelation within Judaism. Kabbalistic writings, like most rabbinic teachings, are based on Torah—on the stories, characters, ethics, and rituals that form the foundation of Jewish tradition.

But where rabbinic interpretations tend toward rational discourse and learned debate, kabbalistic insights stem from a more intuitive meeting between person and text.

One image from kabbalistic literature encourages us to learn to read not only the letters of Torah but also the white spaces around the letters. For the kabbalists, biblical characters often represent various cosmic processes and levels of awareness; rituals reflect universal principles underlying Creation itself; and *mitzvot* (traditional commandments) provide not only a language through which human and Divine communicate, but literally the means to ensure the continuity of Reality. For the kabbalist, Torah is a sourcebook of endless levels of meaning and of meeting.

On a theological level as well, the Jewish mystics differ radically from normative rational rabbinic thought. For the rabbis, God is a Being untouched and unchanged by the created world. For the kabbalists, God participates in creation. God needs humankind as much as humankind needs God—there is a mutuality of relationship in which God participates in all life. *Panentheism* is the term that refers to the mystic's view that there is nowhere that God is not. God is Everywhere and Everything, yet God is also greater than everywhere and everything. God contains the world and is the world, yet God is Infinitely More. God is Being Without Limit. God is the Infinitely Inclusive "I."

The kabbalists believe that we are all participants in the Life of God. Jewish mystical tradition supports the greater awakening to this Inclusivity through study, meditation, and right acts in the world.

The central symbol of the Kabbalah is called the Tree of Life, a map of cosmic, psychological, and spiritual Reality. Two other concepts often related to the Tree are the four worlds of

Creation and the three levels of the soul. Each of these will be touched upon in this text.

Using this Book

This book is designed to allow the greatest flexibility possible while at the same time sustaining a clear focus on a process of authentic spiritual growing. It provides an invitation to personal spiritual expansion that can be used at any time.

You can count back fifty days from a particularly significant moment that is approaching, like a wedding ceremony, birthday, or anniversary, and use the process to encourage greater wakefulness leading to that time. Some have used it to prepare for surgeries, or to support physical healing. Still others have found it helpful to simply open the book at random and "check-in" to the energies and meditations that they discover there.

Creating Your Meditation Journal

A journal of your meditative experiences can be extremely supportive of your practice, allowing you to see more clearly the progression of your development. Note your experiences, your perceptions, and your feelings. Record moments of resistance as well as those of release, stuckness as well as insight.

Regular journal writing helps us all remain more conscious, and helps to support a deepening meditative process. It provides us a natural way to review the stages of our growing as we go along. Over a relatively short time, you will be able to appreciate more clearly your current areas of stuckness as well as the precious moments of liberation you meet.

A Journey of Awakening

An Introduction to the Kabbalistic Tree of Life

The Kabbalistic Tree of Life, or *Eitz Chayim*, is a symbolic representation of the ten levels of reality. The Tree is a model of Creation that provides a graphic response to the question, "If God is One, how come our world looks like it does?" If Reality is One, why do separateness and fragmentation seem so "real"?

The Tree teaches that the nature of "reality" depends upon the place from which that "reality" is viewed. From spaces of "higher" consciousness, Oneness is clear. From spaces of "lower" consciousness, there is clearly separation. It's the same "reality," perceived from different points of view.

The Kabbalistic Tree of Life diagrams the steps through which Consciousness or Energy moves from the highest to the lowest vibrational levels to finally manifest as the physical world we know. This "map of consciousness" provides a model for understanding the nature of all Being as well as the nature of our own particular being. The map guides us in understanding, appreciating, and utilizing all the possible levels, and serves as a foundation for meditative focus. The path downward on the Tree is called the *Path of Creation*, and the path upward describes the *Path of Spiritual Awakening*.

Each level (*sefirah*) of expression on the Tree suggests specific meditative practices that can be approached sequentially or individually. *Sefirah* literally means a *counting*. The Hebrew root of this word also forms the word for "story," and there is a "story" at each of the levels on the Tree of Life.

Each *sefirah* represents a necessary stage in the process through which the Absolute One moves toward manifestation. By analogy, one might imagine that the Tree reflects the flow of electrical energy from the power plant to your home. If the power was directly connected to your house, it would immediately destroy not only all the wiring but even the house itself. So electricity flows from the power plant through a series of transforming stations in which its force is stepped down, so that it enters the home in a usable way.

Energy flows downward through each *sefirah* to express as spiritual, intellectual, emotional, sensational (vibrational), and physical reality. Kabbalistic tradition assigns one of the Names of God to each *sefirah*, and a major biblical character to each of the lower seven *sefirot* (levels). Every *sefirah* is also associated with a part of the human body.

Early kabbalistic teachers first visualized the ten *sefirot* as circles within circles. A ray of light moving into their center indicated the Divine Energy interpenetrating all levels of being.

Sometime in the Middle Ages, these ten levels took on the more familiar configuration that became known as the Tree of Life. This diagram allows greater appreciation of the interactions between the *sefirot*. The basic image suggests the human form, reflecting the notion that each human being expresses the entire Universe in microcosm.

The Basics of the Ten Sefirot and Four Worlds

The Tree of Life diagram as a cosmic map describes how Energy manifests from its least physical state to its most physical. Because most of the *sefirot* received their names from biblical verses, some of their names are not as indicative of their function as one might imagine.

Kabbalistic literature identifies Four Worlds that further describe the unfolding levels of reality. These four levels of reality add to our understanding of how the Tree model functions.

We live in the lowest world, called *Assiyah*, or "doing." Above this world is *Yetzirah*, the World of Formation, then *B'riah*, the World of Creation, and, finally, the highest world called *Atzilut*, the World of Nearness or the World of Emanation. Furthermore, each of them is associated with one of the four letters of the unspeakable Divine "Name," so that the Name of God actually unifies the Four Worlds.

The Tree as we view it in the diagram is actually upside-down. Its roots are in the unmanifest world at the top, and its branches are in the world of manifestation at the bottom. In order to use this image to describe the process of creation, we will refer to the "roots" as the "top" of the Tree, since that is the way the figure looks.

Here are the basic stages through which Creative Energy flows from the top of the Tree to the bottom. The aspects of Creation described by the Tree are related to the spiritual, psychological, emotional, and physical manifestations of human consciousness, since this is the basic model we shall be using in our meditations.

The first *sefirah* at the top, **Keter**, represents the most formless kernel of Consciousness. The journey from unmanifest to manifest passes from **Keter** ("Crown"), to **Chochmah** ("Wisdom"), the vibration of Pure Awareness, or Intuited Awareness. (Remember that whenever Hebrew is transliterated as "ch" the sound is a guttural "kh," as if you are gently clearing your throat.) The first world, called *Atzilut* ("Nearness" or "Emanation"), includes **Keter** and **Chochmah**. This first world is represented by the Hebrew letter, *yod*, the first letter of the Four-Letter Name of God.

The creative flow then proceeds to **Binah** ("Understanding"), the vibration that provides the first form for Awareness (an Ideal or a thought-form). **Binah** contains the second of the four worlds,

B'riah ("Creation"). This second world is represented by the second letter of the Divine Name, the letter *hay*.

The creative flow moves downward across an area called the Abyss, the gap between what is essentially unmanifest and what is essentially manifest, to travel through the next six *sefirot* which together comprise the third world of *Yetzirah* ("Formation"). This world is represented by the letter *vav*, the third letter of the Divine Name. The first of the six *sefirot* in *Yetzirah* is **Chesed** ("Lovingkindness"), where the vibration manifests as emotion. From there, the flow moves to **Gevurah** ("Strength"), the vibration of feeling that provides form for emotional energy.

The Energy achieves balance on the middle pillar of the Tree at **Tiferet** ("Beauty"), the center of the Tree. This middle pillar also represents the levels of identity, and **Tiferet** is the center of Individuated, Inclusive Self-Awareness—our more inclusive identity within which spiritual consciousness awakens.

From **Tiferet**, the flow moves to **Netzach** ("Victory" or "Endurance"), the level of sensory vibration, and then to **Hod** ("Glory"), where the vibration grows more dense to provide the forms of specific sensations and perceptions. The polarity between force and form is balanced again at **Yesod** ("Foundation"), the awakening of individual ego identity.

In the flow of Creation, each *sefirah* below **Keter** receives from above and transmits below, until the final *sefirah*, **Malchut** ("Kingdom"), receives from them all. **Malchut** is the place at which the energies coalesce as the reality we normally experience. This final *sefirah* represents the fourth world of *Assiyah* ("Doing" or "Making"), and is represented by the *hay*, the final letter of the four-letter Name.

The letters of the Name of God unite all worlds and all levels of Being.

Learning the Ten Sefirot

The meditations in this book focus on the lower seven *sefirot*, following the traditional order applied by the sixteenth century kabbalists to the 49-day journey toward awakening. These are the levels for which we humans have greater responsibility. The upper three *sefirot* become available to us as we balance the lower seven.

One of the lower seven *sefirot* is assigned to each of the seven weeks of our journey. Within each week, each day is also assigned a *sefirah*. So every day of the process includes the major focus on the *sefirah* of the week, and an additional focus on the *sefirah* of the day. This will become clearer as you proceed to the actual meditations. The goal is to balance the energies of these seven lower *sefirot* during these seven weeks, but it is helpful to understand how all ten *sefirot* function on the Tree.

The teachers of Kabbalah associated colors and sounds with the *sefirot* to provide additional depth to the meditative experience. As a visualization practice, each *sefirah* can be seen as a sphere of light (although the words "sphere" and "*sefirah*" sound similar, they are not related). The light at each *sefirah* can be imagined according to its color.

The Names of God traditionally assigned to each week are meant as sounds and visualizations for *hitbod'dut*. Associating the particular Name of God at each *sefirah* adds auditory dimensions to the image of the Hebrew letters spelling that name.

The Hebrew vowel sounds associated with specific *sefirot* can be vocalized or sensed in the silence of meditation as extended tones, and the specific vowels can be associated with the letters of the four-letter Name of God. For example, the chant at **Keter** would be "*Yee–Hee–Vee–Hee.*" The four letters can be chanted on a single breath, or each letter can take up a breath, allowing a greater focus on letter and sound.

As might be imagined, there are differences of opinion among kabbalistic teachers regarding the assignment of colors and of vowel sounds to the *sefirot*. Presented here are the sounds and colors that I have found to be most helpful in this meditative process.

The World of Atzilut (Nearness or Emanation)

The upper two *sefirot* make up the world of *Atzilut*, and hold the highest and most inclusive energies. For many kabbalists, *Keter* is not even counted as an actual *sefirah*, since its energy is so undifferentiated. The world of *Atzilut* is beyond our imagination, representing the initial stirrings of Will (*Keter*) and the first rush of Intuition (*Chochmah*) of what will be contained as Pattern, Idea, or Ideal in the world of *B'riah*. Through our spiritual work, we prepare ourselves to be worthy of receiving the gifts of these two highest worlds. The energies of *Atzilut* and *B'riah* may respond to our readiness, but not to our control.

1

כֶּתֶר

KETER
CROWN
The Creative Impulse
Quality of Mind: Will
Part of the Body: Crown of the Head
Identity: The Absolutely Unlimited "I"
Color: Blinding Invisible White
Hebrew Vowel Sound: "Eee" (*Chirik*)
Name of God: EHEYEH ASHER EHEYEH

אֶהְיֶה אֲשֶׁר אֶהְיֶה

I AM as I AM

2

חָכְמָה

CHOCHMAH
WISDOM
The Energy of Awareness
Quality of Mind: Unformed Mental Energy, Intuition
Part of the Body: Right Hemisphere of the Brain
Color: A Gray That Includes All Colors
Hebrew Vowel Sound: "aa" as in "say" (*Tzere*)
Name of God: YAH

יָה

The Eternal

The World of B'riah (Creation)

The second world of *B'riah* ("Creation") contains only the *sefirah* of *Binah*, called the Great Mother. This might be considered the world of Ideal Form, the Unitive model of the universe which will finally manifest at *Malchut*. *Binah* is the Universal Womb, receiving the Universal Seed from *Chochmah*.

3

בִּינָה

BINAH
UNDERSTANDING
The Form of Awareness
Quality of Mind: Ideal Pattern
Part of Body: Left Hemisphere of the Brain
Color: Yellow
Hebrew Vowel Sound: "Ehh" (*Segol*)
Name of God: ELOHIM (Spelled *Yod–Hay–Vav–Hay*)

יהוה

God

The Abyss

When *Keter* is conceived as a non-*sefirah*, the Abyss manifests a *sefirah* to complete the required ten levels on the Tree.

דַּעַת

KNOWLEDGE
Part of the Body: The Third Eye

The World of Yetzirah (Formation)

Yetzirah is the world through which *Binah* connects to *Malchut*. The stages of this World of Formation bring the Formless into form. Remember that the mental level of energy flows downward into this world, so *Yetzirah* reflects the shaping of our level of reality through a progression of mental, emotional, and sensational vibrations.

4

חֶסֶד

CHESED
LOVINGKINDNESS or MERCY
Outpouring of Unformed Emotional Energy
Quality: Ever-flowing Lovingkindness
Part of Body: Right Shoulder
Color: Silver
Hebrew Vowel Sound: "Ahh" (*Patach*)
Name of God: EL

אֵל

God

5

גְּבוּרָה

GEVURAH
SEVERITY or STRENGTH
The Forms of Emotion (Feelings)
Quality: Limitation
Part of Body: Left Shoulder
Color: Gold
Hebrew Vowel Sound: Silent (*Sheva*)
Name of God: ELOHIM

אֱלֹהִים

God

6

תִּפְאֶרֶת

TIFERET
BEAUTY
The "I" of Inclusive Identity
Quality: Compassion, Unconditional Acceptance
Part of Body: The Heart Space
Identity: The Greater Self
Color: Purple
Hebrew Vowel Sound: "Ahh" (*Kamatz*)
Name of God: *Yod-Hay-Vav-Hay* (pronounced *Adonai*)

יהוה

Eternal Being

7

נֶצַח

NETZACH
VICTORY or REVERBERATION
The Force of Physical Sensory Vibration
Quality: Perseverance
Part of Body: Right Solar Plexus (or right leg)
Color: Light Pink
Hebrew Vowel Sound: "Aw" (Short *Kamatz*)
Name of God: ADONAI TZEVA-OT

יהוה צְבָאוֹת

Eternal One of Hosts

8

הוֹד

HOD
GLORY or SPLENDOR
The Form of Sensation
Quality: Beauty of Form
Part of Body: Left Solar Plexus (or left leg)
Color: Dark Pink
Hebrew Vowel Sound: "Oh" (*Cholem*)
Name of God: ELOHIM TZEVA-OT

אֱלֹהִים צְבָאוֹת

God of Hosts

9

יְסוֹד

YESOD
FOUNDATION
Identity: The Separate self
Quality: Foundation of Generative Process
Part of Body: Pubic area
Identity: Ego
Color: Orange
Hebrew Vowel Sound: "OO" (*Shuruk*)
Name of God: EL CHAI or SHADDAI

אֵל חַי   שַׁדַּי

The Living God   The Almighty

The World of Assiyah (Manifesting, Making/Acting)

The final world of *Assiyah*, like the world of *B'riah*, contains a single *sefirah*. Here, *Malchut* receives the flow from the entire Tree, so each *sefirah* is, in fact, reflected in *Malchut*. In this world all the wonders of the Universe are hidden.

10

מַלְכוּת

MALCHUT
KINGDOM or KINGSHIP
Manifest Reality
Identity: Identification with the world
Quality: Actualization
Part of Body: The Base of the Spine (or the Feet)
Color: Blue
Hebrew Vowel Sound: No Vowel (No Vocalization)
The Name of God: ADONAI

אֲדֹנָי

Lord

A Journey of Awakening

Guidelines for Your Practice

There are many ways in which you can use these meditations to support your own unique process. Here are some suggestions you might find helpful.

Remember that a daily practice is most supportive of meditative deepening. It is better to meditate briefly than not to meditate at all. Choose goals that are realistic as well as challenging. The journey of awakening requires that we move beyond our traditional comfort zones.

It is customary to begin the meditation for the day in the evening, when the Jewish day begins, and continue that daily focus until the following sunset.

If you are beginning after Passover, the first week of the counting will begin on the second night of that festival. If your 49-day journey does not coincide with the weeks between Passover and *Shavuot*, you might wish to begin your weekly reading and meditation on Saturday evening or Sunday morning since Sunday is the first day of the Jewish week.

1. Read the weekly meditative reading before reading the meditation of the day. Remember that the basic weekly focus is the foundation for that week.

2. Learn the Name of God for the week, perhaps by copying or tracing the letters and repeating the sound. The Name associated with each week provides a verbal and a visual focus for meditation.

3. Read the meditation of the day and repeat the focus phrases out loud. Feel free to add your own intentions. Remember to use your journal.

ıagine the energy of the weekly sefirah in the appropriate place in your body. Focus on that part of the body, and imagine a radiance of light at that space. Let it glow with the color of that weekly *sefirah*. Experience the energies that awaken within you.

5. Once you sense the *sefirah* of the week, focus on the part of the body associated with the daily *sefirah*, and imagine a radiance of light there. Connect the two with a channel of light. Once again, experience the energies that awaken within you.

6. Chant, either aloud or silently, the vowel sound of the *sefirah* of the week. Place this vowel after each of the letters of the Four-Letter Name of God. For example, during the first week the chant would be *Yahh–Hahh–Vahh–Hahh*.

7. Focus on the specific quality or energy represented by the weekly *sefirah*, and consider that aspect of your experience. Pay attention to how the energies of the daily *sefirah* are experienced. Discover the relationships between the *sefirot* and your perceptions that day.

8. You might want to share this process with others, so you can support each other and deepen your experience through that sharing. Having a "meditation buddy" can help us stay on track and learn from each other.

9. Open to the spirit of adventure. There is no way of knowing in advance what wonders will open for you in your steps from enslavement to freedom. Each time you engage this process of awakening, your experience will be different.

Ritual for Counting the Days of this Omer Journey

The traditional Counting of the Omer includes the following blessing, recited in the evening (or during *ma'ariv*, the evening worship service), followed by the counting itself. When you are practicing these meditations during the actual days between Passover and *Shavuot*, the meditations follow the blessing and the counting.

Our blessings themselves become meditations when they flow with *kavannah*, with "intentionality" and "one-pointed attention." Savor the blessing. Let it speak through the Heart of your Inner Silence. Be receptive to the meanings it holds.

The Blessing Preceding the Counting

בָּרוּךְ אַתָּה יהוה אֱלֹהֵינוּ מֶלֶךְ הָעוֹלָם
אֲשֶׁר קִדְּשָׁנוּ בְּמִצְוֹתָיו וְצִוָּנוּ עַל סְפִירַת הָעוֹמֶר.

Baruch Atah Adonai, Eloheynu Melech ha-olam,
asher kid'shanu b'mitz'votav v'tzivanu ahl s'firat ha-Omer.

Blessed are You, Eternal One our God, Universal Creative Presence, Who sanctifies us with paths of holiness and gives us this path of counting the days of Omer.

The Formula for Counting the 49 Days of the Omer Journey

Today is the ___ day,
[comprising ___ weeks and ___ days]
of the Omer.

A Journey of Awakening

Forty-Nine Steps

on this

Journey of Awakening

A Journey of Awakening

The First Week
at Chesed:

The Flow of Lovingkindness

I take moments of quiet each day this week to simply appreciate the fuller nature of my experience. I especially notice the abundant flow of Life behind all my feelings. This week I discover the abundant outpouring of possibility.

The Sefirah of the Week

Chesed is often perceived as the "favorite" *sefirah* on the Tree of Life. It is seen as the place where the energies of Lovingkindness flow without limit. Another name for **Chesed** is **Gedolah**, which means "largesse," or "greatness."

Chesed reflects the flow of energy before it can be limited as specific feelings at **Gevurah**. Not yet differentiated, this energy radiates Life-force. This flow of Life-force will later manifest as both positive and negative feelings, but at this point the flow precedes any polarity. This is the Light behind both the light and shadow at **Gevurah**. The *sefirah* of force on the right side of the Tree expresses energy before it separates into the polarities brought about through particular forms.

The negative as well as the positive feelings to manifest at **Gevurah** are both evidence of the unitive flow of emotional energy from **Chesed**, yet we yearn to meet the ever-flowing abundance of **Chesed** without the restrictions at **Gevurah**. This first week of the journey calls us to open ourselves, to receive from the Fountain of Life, and to be nourished.

The Name of God

At **Chesed**, the Name of God is *El*, "God." *El* appears as if it were the singular noun which becomes the plural form *Elohim* at **Gevurah**, even though the words are not linguistically related in that way. The name reflects the energy of this *sefirah*, since **Chesed** presents an abundant flow of that which is not yet differentiated into multiple specific feelings.

Traditionally, *El* is understood to reflect the Universal attributes of Compassion and Mercy. Yet this kind of mercy and compassion is not the same as the *feelings* that arise at **Gevurah**. At **Chesed**, Mercy represents the ever-flowing, ever-providing, ever-sustaining Energy of unlimited abundance and possibility.

El signifies the Energy which shall later infuse *Elohim*. *El* offers Itself without reservation, and in that sense is truly Merciful and Loving.

This Name of God in Scripture

And You, Eternal One, are *El*, full of Compassion, Gracious, Long-suffering, and Bountiful in Loving-kindness and Truth.

(Psalm 86:15)

The Meditative Focus

Each feeling we experience is itself a shell through which we can meet the grander not-yet-limited flow of Divine Energy. We release ourselves to the abundance of that offering, drinking fully at the Fountain of Life now available to us.

Guidelines for Intentions in the First Week at Chesed

not planning the
being in moment

We begin every true journey without a clear image of where we wish to be. From a place of stuckness, it is not possible to know the Promised Land. *Mitzrayim* is the ancient kingdom of Egypt, but now it represents our self-enslavements. Perhaps all enslavements are self-enslavements, reflected in negative self-statements, negative judgments of others, and negative messages about our world. *Mitzrayim* at this moment manifests as each place of stuckness in our lives.

From the place of self-limitation, from the place of contraction, it is not possible to know the goals which unfold only through self-expansion. Every time we think we know the answer to our problems from the level of those problems themselves, we discover that answer to be surprisingly short-lived.

So the journey begins with **Chesed**, the *sefirah* of the ever-flowing, over-flowing, totally accepting Energy of emotion. This Flow shall be totally accepting of the forms offered next week at **Gevurah**. But this week celebrates **Chesed,** so we honor the Energies with which we are nourished.

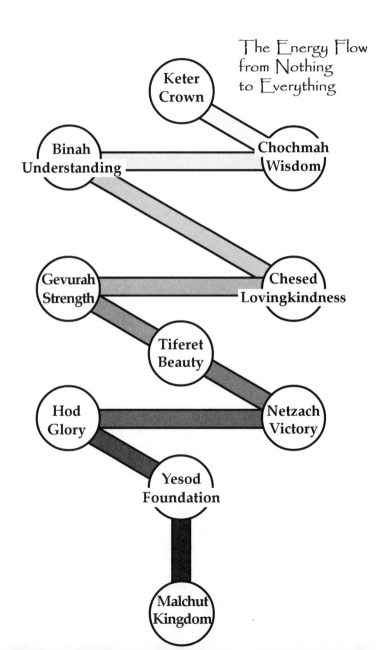

The Energy Flow
from Nothing
to Everything

Keter
Crown

Chochmah
Wisdom

Binah
Understanding

Gevurah
Strength

Chesed
Lovingkindness

Tiferet
Beauty

Hod
Glory

Netzach
Victory

Yesod
Foundation

Malchut
Kingdom

Meditation for the First Day

Our challenge is to choose freedom. With freedom comes true life. With slavery comes the pretense of life. The journey from slavery to freedom is filled with wonder and challenges us to step beyond our past. Slavery is the stuckness in our lives that can carry great pain; it is the paralysis that brings a kind of deadness. This kind of enslavement separates us from our fuller possibilities and convinces us of our limitations. Our memory of historical slavery is a metaphor for the inner slavery that we experience still.

The paradox of slavery is that it is safe. The world is predictable, and there is security in being able to blame the external world for the problems we experience.

Each day of our counting we focus on two *sefirot*, two energy levels on the kabbalistic Tree of Life: the *sefirah* of the week and the *sefirah* of the day. Today we begin the week of **Chesed**, the *sefirah* of Lovingkindness, of Emotional Energy. And this first day brings **Chesed** into **Chesed**. We begin our journey focusing on the sphere of Light at the right shoulder. And we release ourselves to this Energy of Lovingkindness.

Freedom allows us to expand. When we are free, we are free to choose, and free to change ourselves and our world. Yet with greater freedom comes greater responsibility. There is an awesome quality to our true freedom, for with greater freedom we are able to respond more fully to ourselves, to each other, and to our world. A deep inner security then replaces our dependence on external circumstances that we often use to suppress change.

Our Omer Journey is a metaphor for our personal journey from the confines of our current self-definitions to the wonder of renewed self-creation. This is the task to which we are called. The Life of this Universe calls each of us to the fullness of our own life. In this way we participate in Creation itself.

Daily Focus:

I step beyond the safe confines of my enslavements now. I am filled with exactly the energies I need as I begin my journey toward greater purpose and meaning. I welcome this deep Lovingkindness that naturally supports my growing.

Like a silver flute - an open reed accepting This energy moving through me. Restorative

Aware of how tired I was after 2nd Seder last night - resisting opening to Chesed because I feared it would propel me into more action but the pure quality Chesed in Chesed is filling

35

Meditation for the Second Day

The true journey from slavery to freedom begins slowly. There is far to go. Yet we begin with the energies upon which true freedom is always based. Into this week of **Chesed**, the Emotional Energies called Lovingkindness, we bring **Gevurah**, the *sefirah* of Emotional Form. In our meditations, we experience the channel of Light connecting the right shoulder with the left shoulder.

We tend to appreciate energy more readily than we do the limitation of that energy, yet without limitation no energy can express in meaningful ways. We welcome **Gevurah**, which is the symbol of Limitation on the Tree, that we might effectively express the Lovingkindness of **Chesed**. Our emotions bridge the gap between operations of mind and expressions of body. From emotions come our feelings, which are the valuations we place on our perceptions of self and the world. And from those valuations come our commitments and our pursuits.

We seek the Emotional Forms that will most effectively contain the Emotional Force available to us. We seek to remain flexible at **Gevurah** so that we can respond most appropriately to the offerings that flow from **Chesed**.

The crucial connection between **Chesed** and **Gevurah** is affirmed today. This connection provides the foundation for the next steps in the creative process.

Our emotions can express through both destructive as well as healing forms. Our challenge is to allow Emotional Force to express most fully by honoring emotional forms expressing greater love and compassion.

Daily Focus:

I honor both the energy and the form of emotional expression now. I relax body and mind, and trust the higher energies to manifest through me in supportive and healing ways. I receive more fully now, that I might express more effectively in my world.

3 Meditation for the Third Day

On this third day of our process, we seek the balance of **Tiferet** in **Chesed**. **Tiferet** is the Heart Space, translated as "Beauty." It is the *sefirah* symbolizing the energies of the Greater Self, the Individuated "I."

The Greater Self that lives within each one of us is drawn this day into the field of Lovingkindness. We receive from this outpouring of emotion that which supports the fuller awakening of our deeper Self. And, in turn, this Self contributes to the reality of **Chesed** itself.

The central pillar of the Tree provides the place of balance between force and form. The basic identities through which we awaken are represented on this central pillar, from the ego self to the inclusive Self to the Unlimited Self. The Tree reflects the function of identity: it is through the individual that the *tikkun olam*, the great healing, must express in the world. The Tree of Identity, which is the central pillar of the Tree of Life, speaks to the essential nature of the spiritual journey in which we open from the inside-out to the wonders of the One we are.

We experience these *sefirot* as glowing spheres of energy at our right shoulder and at our heart space, and feel the connection between the two. The heart opens to receive and to transmit the balance it contains, and this deeper centering infuses the energy at **Chesed.**

Daily Focus:

Within my heart I meet the deeper message of Love to be expressed through word and deed. I honor the Compassion brought this day into the flow of Lovingkindness. I feel the light of Lovingkindness illuminate my entire being, as I breathe these universal rhythms deeply. I am nourished by the compassionate flow of Life awakening within me now. In this fuller awareness, I grow and I share.

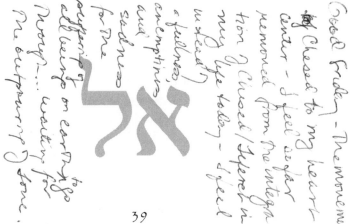

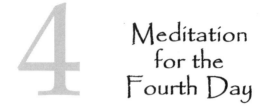

Meditation for the Fourth Day

We live in **Chesed** this week, filling ourselves with the energies which are seeking expression through us. We are the beings charged with the responsibility of bringing heaven and earth together. And today **Chesed**, Lovingkindness, finally connects more closely to the physical energies which will manifest as the physical reality in which we live.

Today **Netzach**, Victory or Reverberation, experienced on the right side of the solar plexus, is brought into **Chesed**. **Chesed** is the *sefirah* holding fully expressive emotional energies. **Netzach** is the *sefirah* holding fully expressive physical energies.

Feel the connection from right shoulder to right solar plexus. The right side of the body is illuminated, radiating energies of Lovingkindness and physical vitality. Both **Chesed** and **Netzach** are on the right side of the Tree, so we become more aware of the flow and the force of Energy.

There is an eternal quality about the Energy of this day, and we know this force is contained within every thought, feeling, and sensation. Prior to the limitations of particular form, all things are possible. So today we open to the awareness of that possibility in our own lives and in our own world.

Daily Focus:

I experience the radiating emotional and physical vitality that fills me now with renewed possibility and purpose. I appreciate these gifts that live through me. I bless them, and discover new and fuller ways to express them in my world. There are no limits to the energies now available. Today I honor the new possibilities for self and for world.

אל

The meeting of Heaven and Earth in human form — my body, the Body of Christ, The cross

Meditation for the Fifth Day

Today we link **Chesed**, the outpouring of Lovingkindness, with **Hod**, "Glory," the container that shines with the beauty of those energies. **Hod** represents physical form as known through our sensations and perceptions. These forms provide containers through which the energies from **Netzach** can express. The *sefirot* for today radiate in the body at the right shoulder and the left side of the solar plexus.

The Universal seeks to express Itself in the material world. That Which Is Without Limit seeks to manifest through that which is always limited. And we who span both realities seek to remember which is which.

How often we grow confused. We begin to cherish the form, and glorify the container. We forget that the true meaning of all form derives from that which is contained. In our forgetting, we create shells whose beauty threatens to dissolve before our very eyes.

Too often we focus on these external forms, striving to shore them up without attending to the energies that in fact give them their glory. We ourselves cannot help but become caught in this dilemma. The forms that hold the Spirit of Lovingkindness will reflect that beauty most truly when we recognize them for what they truly are. This day of bringing **Hod** into **Chesed** challenges us to remember where the beauty really resides.

Daily Focus:

My sensations embody Lovingkindness. Through every sensation this Lovingkindness manifests. Today I perceive this Lovingkindness reflected in every perception, and know the blessing of the One Who gives all life its beauty and its glory.

Alleluia, Alleluia, Alleluia - The Christ is Risen. The Christ-consciousness - now is the Chesed. The Hod is the glorious form of Jesus and the many teachers I've learned from. All Thanks to Jesus, the angels and my parents, Mrs. Tom, Will, Frank, Keating, Cumer, Young, Cecilia, Bill, Denis, Dennis, Chernin, Prema, Laura Yogananda, Harry V. Vekirlands, Rabbi Kushner, Jerry, yoga George, Randy and my children and all other teachers - Annie Rose, Judy, Friedman, Mickey, Ron, Mary Anne, Lynn, Anita, Sue brothers and sisters, too many to list - Thanks be to God!

43

Meditation for the Sixth Day

The sixth day of this meditative process brings the *sefirah* **Yesod,** "Foundation," into **Chesed. Yesod** is centered at the genitals and represents the ego identity in all its glories and all its limitations. This area of body and this aspect of self are today invited into the energy of Lovingkindness symbolized by **Chesed.** The right shoulder and the genitals are connected by a channel of radiant light and energy.

We need the ego to support our survival as separate biological and psychological entities in the world so that we can express the energies that are available to us. But that ego identity easily forgets that which gives it deeper life and deeper meaning, and imagines it is here all by itself.

Chesed, the center of Lovingkindness, needs **Yesod** to carry its energies into the world, and **Yesod** needs **Chesed** in order to remember the deeper Nature of its being. All the *sefirot* are interdependent. In the Kabbalistic scheme, the world needs all ten to exist. Each *sefirah* represents an essential aspect of the Creation process, just as each represents an essential aspect of the process of spiritual awakening.

As **Yesod** is held in **Chesed**, it is blessed with the fullness of Energy at that *sefirah*. Today the unlimited flow of Lovingkindness meets and blesses our lesser self. **Yesod** brings the personal identity, through whom all Creation will be met, into **Chesed**, the Lovingkindness which seeks that realization.

Daily Focus:

All that I am is blessed by the Universal Energy of Lovingkindness. Through every cell of my being this Lovingkindness awakens, and I perceive with greater clarity the One Whose Life expresses everywhere. As I recognize the Life that flows through all being, I am better able to express Lovingkindness in my world.

אל

Loving kindness with Ego
Identity - awsomw to banj of
how self-interest allways
asserts itself first — in a
hurry wanting to be taken
care of now

Meditation for the Seventh Day

Our focus this first week has been at **Chesed**, the *sefirah* of Lovingkindness. Each day of the week, we brought the energies of one of the lower seven *sefirot* into **Chesed**. This seventh day brings **Malchut**, the "Kingdom," the "lowest" of the manifestations of energy on the Tree of Life, into **Chesed**. The highest and the lowest of the seven *sefirot* of our meditations are joined today. They will meet again on the first day of the seventh week, when the "host" *sefirah* will have reversed, and **Malchut** will welcome **Chesed**.

Now the energies of the world of our experience moves into **Chesed** to balance the Tree there, for each *sefirah* contains an entire Tree. In turn, the fullness of **Chesed** connects today to this world. In **Malchut** all the flavors of the upper vessels manifest, but the Holy is hidden in husks of materiality. Today, this space is held in the Lovingkindness of **Chesed**, as **Malchut** provides a grounding for the fullness of **Chesed**.

Our meditations for this day focus on the energies of the *sefirot* at the right shoulder and the base of the spine, and the channel of light connecting them. The *sefirah* of Lovingkindness welcomes the *sefirah* of the "real" world.

If you are doing this process following Passover, this is the final day of its observance. Tomorrow evening we enjoy fresh *chametz*, bread made again with leavening. The ancient metaphor speaks to the healing that is accomplished through this first week of meditative focusing. We are renewing our awareness of the multi-dimensionality of our being, and opening ourselves to an ever-expanding journey.

Daily Focus:

I grow more aware of the Presence of Lovingkindness in which this world is held. I feel this deeper influence through every cell of my being. I am always one with this Universal Source of Life. All reality reflects this Loving Presence. In all I meet, I sense the blessing of this Love.

God's yearning love for us - always seeking + pursuing us... aware of how that love suffuses all.

A Journey of Awakening

The Second Week at Gevurah:

אלהים

Setting Limits

As I remember to breathe gently, I am able to notice more carefully the nature of my experience at this moment. I become more aware now of the feelings that are attached to all my thoughts and sensations. Each feeling limits emotional energy and allows it to be experienced.

The Sefirah of the Week

Gevurah, "Strength," is the most problematic *sefirah* on the Tree of Life. It is generally seen as the *sefirah* of Judgment, since another traditional name for this *sefirah* is **Din**, which literally means "judgment." **Gevurah** is on the left side of the Tree and so represents form, and within the world of form unfold the polarities of our experience. **Gevurah** represents the forms called "feelings," forms which contain and limit emotional energy. With **Gevurah** comes happiness as well as sadness, pleasure as well as pain. We cannot know one without the other. So **Gevurah** is seen as the origin of "evil," since it is the place where we first feel "good."

The very first *sefirah* on the left side of the Tree is **Binah**, but it is at **Gevurah** that true distinction and polarity arises. At **Binah**, the form which arises to hold the flow from **Chochmah** is still Unitive. Not until emotional form is present can polarity truly be known.

The Name of God

At **Gevurah**, the Name of God is *Elohim*, "God." *Elohim* is the Name associated with judgment and with severity, and so is associated with this *sefirah*. In Jewish tradition, the two most often used names of God are *Elohim* and *Yod–Hay–Vav–Hay* (pronounced *Adonai*). *Elohim* is translated, "God," and

50

Yod–Hay–Vav–Hay is generally rendered, "Lord," or more literally translated, "The Eternal."

Elohim is actually the plural form of the noun, yet it is virtually always translated as if it was singular, and takes a singular verb and modifier. One way of explaining this is to understand **Elohim** as the One Being (*Yod–Hay–Vav–Hay*) appearing to our awareness as the many. **Elohim** can be appreciated as the Indwelling Presence of *Yod–Hay–Vav–Hay* within each individual being.

This Indwelling Presence is called **Shechinah**, which is also another name given for **Elohim**, as stated in the thirteenth century Jewish mystical text called the *Zohar* and elsewhere.

This Name of God in Scripture

Be still, and know that I AM *Elohim*.

(Psalm 46:11)

The Meditative Focus

Always begin with a breath of relaxation, then gently become aware of the current nature of your experience in the world. Focus on the feelings you find, learning to appreciate them without judgment.

This entire meditative journey calls us to step more fully into the immediacy of the present moment. As we attend gently and persistently to the contents of our awareness, each moment naturally expands. There is so much more here than we had been noticing.

Our feelings bring us joy and bring us sadness. Yet beyond their particularity, we can learn much simply from the way in which feelings arise within us.

Guidelines for Intentions in the Second Week at Gevurah

Gevurah is the *sefirah* that takes the heat. It is seen as the place of limitation, the place at which cold-heartedness enters the world. **Gevurah** contains the whispers of evil, of the "other side." But what **Gevurah** does, a function requiring a good deal of "strength," is to *realize* **Chesed**. Not until a feeling takes shape can we experience the powerful world of emotion. Each feeling is itself a limitation of the wonderful flow of Life from **Chesed**. We fight against the limitations, and so we become stuck in them. We get so caught in well-worn feelings, in roles and scripts defining who we are and how we are in the world, that we close ourselves off from the adventure of our growing.

Gevurah itself is not the problem. The problem is our own tendency to cling to our favorite feelings, mostly bewailing them. When we refuse to let them go, we block the energies of **Chesed** from flowing more freely into our world.

The secret of **Gevurah** is that it is the place where polarities are born—polarities of good and bad, up and down, higher and lower, better and worse. Polarities enter the world at **Gevurah**, for polarities are the consequences of emotion made feeling. The way that feeling limits, holds, and shapes emotional energy almost automatically creates its opposite, for feelings are known by their opposites. Without "easy," we would not appreciate "difficult." Without "boredom," we would be unable to identify "excitement."

Gevurah provides the stuff of our dreams and of our nightmares both. This week, we focus on the forms of our feelings, noticing and celebrating the polarities they bring. There is no need to resist any feeling, because when feelings are more fully accepted, they reveal themselves and then shift.

Meditation for the Eighth Day

Counting the Omer is a metaphor for counting the steps on the journey from slavery to freedom, from unconsciousness to full awareness. The journey, of course, is never quite that simple. We are not coming from total unconsciousness, nor are we opening now to total awareness. Yet our task is to meet the challenge of becoming more aware of the Life which is our life, of the freedom which is ours. And so we begin a second week of the journey.

This second week focuses on **Gevurah**, that *sefirah* placed at the left shoulder which balances **Chesed** on the right side. **Gevurah** by itself can symbolize the dark side, the *sitra achra*, the place of evil. It holds the possibility of being mere shell without energy. It is the place of shadows without light. It is the place of restriction and of contraction, since its energies limit the pure flow from **Chesed**. Because it provides a form for **Chesed**, it allows that Lovingkindness to manifest as feeling. Because any form limits **Chesed**, it threatens to strangle the very energies for which it is a vessel. At **Gevurah** we sense most clearly the essential paradox of all form.

Since **Gevurah** is the *form* of emotional energy, our task is to better recognize and appreciate the feelings which arise within us. This first day of the second week brings **Chesed** into **Gevurah**, to help us sense the presence of that Lovingkindness within all the feelings we experience.

This week we focus on the left shoulder, and today imagine a channel of light between the illuminations at left and right shoulder. Notice that the channel passes through the throat, illuminating that center of expression and creativity. With this energy, we enter with greater awareness into our experience this day.

Daily Focus:

I awaken to a new reverence for all the feelings which arise in me now. I grow more aware than ever that the energy of Lovingkindness animates all feelings. This awareness helps me appreciate the incredible dance of feelings I experience. I begin this second week with blessing.

Meditation for the Ninth Day

Our focus this week at the *sefirah* of **Gevurah**, symbolically manifesting in the body at the left shoulder, draws us to a greater awareness of our feelings. The second day of each week of this process brings **Gevurah** into the *sefirah* of the week, so today is **Gevurah** in **Gevurah**.

Emotion has to do with the energy behind our feelings, so **Gevurah** is the *sefirah* representing the *form* of that energy. Today we are called to awaken with less resistance to the feelings in which we carry our emotional energy. All our patterns and our roles help limit the feelings we are able to experience. But no matter what our feelings, **Gevurah** allows us to know them.

Often we tend to resist our habitual negative feelings, but what we resist grows even stronger. To encourage our own expansion, it is necessary to honor all those forms which we find ourselves expressing. To step beyond our yesterdays, we need to take responsibility for our past choices, and accept them. Then we might move beyond them.

To honor the current emotional expressions of our energies is the challenge of this day. Such acceptance is the key that frees us from old cycles of experience and expression. When we honor ourselves and our past creations, we bring new flexibility into those forms that they might expand with fuller Life.

Daily Focus:

I become aware of any feelings of self-condemnation I carry. I know that I am a creative being, experiencing through my feelings the Greater Creative Presence Who lives in me and as me. When I accept my current experience, I allow an expansion of feelings. New forms emerge to express deeper levels of my own integrity. I welcome the fuller flow of Creative energies now.

Meditation for the Tenth Day

Yesterday brought **Gevurah** into this week of **Gevurah**, bringing us up against the emotional forms of our current creations and encouraging our appreciation of the necessity of such forms.

This tenth day brings **Tiferet** into **Gevurah**, so the *sefirah* of Limitation welcomes the *sefirah* of Compassion. **Tiferet** brings its fountain of calmness into **Gevurah**, and we are elevated to a greater awareness. With the energies of **Tiferet**, we can know that the emotional forms in our lives have been perfectly conceived to allow us to grow on this journey we have chosen for ourselves.

It is this deep Compassion, this deep knowing, that allows **Gevurah** the flexibility to welcome greater energies as we proceed on our journey of awakening. As we feel the inner connection of light between the left shoulder and the heart, there is a releasing of that which had been bound up. There is a relaxing of old judgments; there is again an opening.

We can feel a dawning of wonder when what was closed now opens again. New Light springs forth from the shadows of our lives. This day allows us to meet ourselves anew. Energies of possibility again greet us.

Life pulses its vitality into the world through every cell of our beings. The Heart of Life throbs within our chests, Life's Breath breathes us. Through every action or dream or thought or deed, this Life moves through us. Life is an interaction, a co-operation, an interdependence. Life moves, shifts, and expands through us.

Daily Focus:

Today what was closed opens again. New possibilities awaken with the day, as I experience a renewed sense of wonder at the expansion I feel deeply within. I discover a fountain of Compassion that nourishes the fuller expression of my Being. In this Compassion, I discover forms of feeling more inviting for the energies of openness and Oneness. There is new joy in this day.

Meditation for the Eleventh Day

As multi-dimensional beings, we walk an ancient wilderness at the very same time that we live our lives here and now. Our journey calls us to balance more deeply the energies which give us Life and Purpose. And so this eleventh step, this day of bringing **Netzach** into **Gevurah**. This day we let the Light connect the left shoulder with the right side of the solar plexus.

Gevurah gives shape to the emotional outpouring of **Chesed** that it might realize itself in the world. **Netzach** symbolizes those energies, lower down on the Tree, which will later express through our perceptions of the physical realm. The channel of Light in our visualization today crosses through **Tiferet**, and is blessed by that center of compassionate awareness, that our physical vitality might be experienced with greater integrity and meaning.

We are urged to give special attention to the vibrational energies which flow through us and which are not yet manifest. Reverberations which have not yet appeared as perceptions and sensations are brought into **Gevurah** now. Within this week of limitation comes the incredible vitality of this almost-realized persistent vital aliveness.

Gevurah balances itself this week, bringing in each of the other seven *sefirot*. Today **Gevurah** meets the energy which has been birthed through her, and perhaps appreciates more fully the implications of its role.

Daily Focus:

This day I honor the energies of Life which fill me. I am aware of the feelings associated with the vitality of physical energy. I am revitalized as I meet the energies I experience. My actions in the world now more energetically reflect the Life which infuses all things.

אלהים

Why is it so hard to get Gevurah? This week I'm struggling under — standing. So I simplify to the purist, color, name of God & go with that. Now the breadth is in limiting, or accepting limits

Meditation
for the
Twelfth Day

Today our focus is on the left side of the Tree of Life. The connection is experienced between **Gevurah** at the left shoulder and **Hod** at the left side of the solar plexus. As **Gevurah** symbolically provides form for the emotional energies from **Chesed**, so **Hod** provides specific sensations and perceptions as forms for the physical energies flowing from **Netzach**. **Hod** is "Glory," the fulfillment of physical sensation and perception.

Energies spring forth into the world through the forms provided them on the left side of the Tree. Form differentiates that energy so it can be experienced mentally, emotionally, and physically. But when that form grows rigid, it inhibits expansion.

All forms grow rigid. That is the nature of form. All energies can overwhelm. That is the nature of force.

In this day of focusing on form, we become better able to appreciate that our negative judgments keeps forms rigid. Blessing allows flexibility.

So we seek to bless the feelings and the sensations we are manifesting, that we might become more than we now are. Each feeling, each sensation, and each perception is a wonder in itself.

Daily Focus:

I release the constraints of self-condemnation now. I surround myself with the Light of Being and experience the radiance of blessing through every cell of my body. The feelings which flow through me support wholeness and healing. I experience my feelings and my sensations expressing more freely now.

Meditation for the Thirteenth Day

The number thirteen is a good omen in Jewish tradition. It is the *gematria*, the sum of the numerical value of the Hebrew letters, of the word *Echad*, which means "One," as well as the *gematria* of *Ahavah*, which means "Love." Added together, the words "One" and "Love" equal twenty-six, which is also the *gematria* of the four-letter unspeakable Name of God: *Yod–Hay–Vav–Hay*, for which we read the word *Adonai*. So there are special energies available to us now in this journey of awakening.

Today we bring the energies of **Yesod** into **Gevurah**. **Yesod** is the "Foundation," the place of ego-identity, energetically located at the genitals in the human body. We imagine the channel of light connecting the left shoulder and the pubic area. We bring our ego into the place of Limitation to seek its proper form. Ego is always in need of higher energy as well as more effective structure. And **Yesod** brings the Foundation of personal identity into the realm of **Gevurah**, so that *sefirah* might know the nature of the identity who carries Holy Energy into the world.

Placed at the area of the genitals, **Yesod** reflects the influences of sexuality. Our ego identity is largely bound up in our sexuality, in the challenge not only to act in the world with sexual integrity, but to balance within each of us the energies of male and female.

Yesod is the center of the soul which the *Zohar*, the thirteenth century major text of the Kabbalah, calls the *nefesh*. It is the animal soul. The *nefesh* cut off from higher energies is separate and competitive; the *nefesh* receiving from its Source connects that Source consciously to this realm.

In *nefesh* we know the pain of separateness, the powerlessness of our separate self when collapsed in alienation from others and from the world. Yet we grow to respect the integrity of our separate selves as we move beyond the notion that this realm is all there is and allow the influences of a deeper awareness to express more fully.

Yesod moves into **Gevurah** to receive the blessing of its proper form.

Daily Focus:

I am filled with deep respect for the expression of my uniqueness in the world. I am aware of the value of form which allows me to move and act in the world. My mind, my emotions, and my body serve as vehicles for Being. I am whole and I am complete now.

14 Meditation for the Fourteenth Day

We are concluding our second week of the journey. The week in **Gevurah** ends by bringing in **Malchut**, the lowest *sefirah*. The channel of Light reaches from the left shoulder to the base of the spine.

Malchut is the "Kingdom." It is the *sefirah* of our earthly existence, receiving the energies from the entire Tree. In most kabbalistic writings, it is the place of the Indwelling Presence, called *Shechinah*, the Feminine aspect of the One. In kabbalistic metaphor, it is our task to realize *Shechinah* in this realm, that we might support the reintegration of Holy Energies.

Malchut seems like the land of limitations. It is the place in which we can go unconscious and lose ourselves. And at the same time, it is the place of our awakening responsibility. We are the beings who are called upon to remember Wholeness in this land of forgetting. We are the ones with the freedom to awaken in the land of the sleepers.

This whole week in **Gevurah** has been filled with the challenge to realize the perfection of limitation, to perceive the appropriateness of the forms through which the One might speak. In **Malchut** we are faced with forms that seem silent, so it is our task to learn to listen more carefully, to become receptive to that which is hidden right in front of our eyes.

Malchut brings to **Gevurah** the ultimate expression of its form. Perhaps **Malchut** urges **Gevurah** to hold less tightly to the structures it creates, that the worlds which follow might know deeper inspiration for growth and evolution.

Each of the seven weeks of our counting concludes with the focus at **Malchut**. If we can balance ourselves here, we can bring heaven and earth together. We seek to bring balance within ourselves, to balance our internal heaven and earth, our inner tensions of awareness and forgetting. So the last day of this week holds special promise. In our meditations, we celebrate greater awakening of **Malchut** in **Gevurah**.

Daily Focus:

I release my insistence that things be other than they are, that I might realize the blessings hidden within the events of my life. There are higher forms which now manifest through me and around me, to hold more fully the energies of Holiness flowing from their Source. I feel a deeper sense of Peace and Love reflecting through the world which is my home.

A Journey of Awakening

The Third Week
at Tiferet:

יהוה

Balance in the Breath of Compassion

I remember the silence within, I remember to breathe
gently, and I simply accept my experience of this
moment. I discover the space of my Expanded Identity
when I breathe a Universal Breath. I am a precious
expression of a Universal Identity.

The Sefirah of the Week

Tiferet is the Center of the Tree of Life. The right side of the Tree signifies force, and the left side, form. The central pillar symbolizes balance and identity. The identity at **Tiferet** is the "Inclusive I," the inclusive shared-Self behind the exclusive ego-self.

In **Tiferet**, there is a balance between the self which resides in the body and the Universal Self beyond individuation. Here the worlds are connected.

At **Tiferet** there is also a balance of force and form. **Tiferet** is the "heart-space" of the Tree, reflected as the heart-space within each of us. **Tiferet** holds an ever-expanding Compassionate Awareness.

The Name of God

יהוה

The Name of God at **Tiferet** is pronounced *Adonai*, but is written *Yod–Hay–Vav–Hay*. This Name is not pronounced as written because it points to That Which Is Beyond Name.

This four-letter Name is known as the tetragrammaton ("four-letter name"), and whenever it appears in the Hebrew Bible or in prayer texts, we pronounce the word *Adonai*. It is important to remember that *Adonai* is a totally different word which more literally translates as "Eternal Being."

The Name ‏יהוה‏ (*Yod–Hay–Vav–Hay*), is a form of the Hebrew verb which means "to be," and so can be translated, "Unlimited Being." That is why many of us translate *Yod–Hay–Vav–Hay* (when we *see* the letters *Yod–Hay–Vav–Hay* but *say Adonai*) as "The Eternal One," or "The Eternal Presence." The more common translation of *Adonai* as "Lord" is more specifically the translation of the actual word *Adonai*.

This Name of God in Scripture

I set ‏יהוה‏ (*Yod–Hay–Vav–Hay* read as *Adonai*) before me always.

(Psalm 6:8)

The Meditative Focus

Now we allow ourselves to awaken to a greater sense of balance. There is a peacefulness which expands within the Heart of our being, a peacefulness which gradually radiates through our consciousness. We open to an awareness that holds compassion for everything it touches.

Guidelines for Intentions in the Third Week at Tiferet

Tiferet is the Heart of the Tree. It provides a central focus, a place of balance. There are even some representations of the Tree which have each of the other *sefirot,* except **Malchut,**

directly connected to **Tiferet** at the center. **Tiferet** is a place of balance between **Chesed** and **Gevurah,** and between **Netzach** and **Hod**. It is the place of balance between **Malchut** and **Keter**.

The central pillar of the Tree represents not only balance, but identity. The identity at this *sefirah* is the "Inclusive I" of the Self. It is this identity which mediates between the individual consciousness of the ego and the unlimited Universal Self beyond.

If the central pillar is the place of balance, it must also be the place of tension. **Tiferet** is asked to remain open to both force and form, to avoid the seductions of the limitlessness flow of Consciousness, as well as the attractive safety of form. Compassion is the quality that awakens at **Tiferet**—the willingness to receive everything that exists with the equanimity of true acceptance.

The breath is one of the keys to opening this **Tiferet**-awareness. The Zohar urges, "Breathe like the ocean rises and falls and never becomes full." The breath is received and released fully—expansion and contraction—all in the service of Life.

Meditation for the Fifteenth Day

The third week of our journey focuses on the *sefirah* of **Tiferet**, the Heart Center, the place of Compassion. Here Energy and Form find balance, and Heaven and Earth meet. We feel Tiferet awaken with the full glow of Light in our own heart space.

On any significant journey, our energies tend to dim as we go. Like our ancestors, there are parts of ourselves which automatically bring our own favorite limitations into this wilderness, so we may notice our determination begin to waver. This week invites us to reassess the journey, to remember our purpose, to renew our resolve.

Only at Tiferet can we find united that which our senses continually separate. Tiferet is the center of our higher Identity, our non-ego awareness. Where the "I" at Yesod is exclusive, the "I" at Tiferet is inclusive. Tiferet is the place of the soul our tradition calls *ruach*, the Identity within us which mediates communication between our highest Self, *neshamah*, and our body self, the *nefesh*.

Ruach is the place of breath, and it is with the relaxed and balanced breath that we naturally become more aware of the energies of the heart. The level of soul called *ruach* awakens within the larger "I" of our Being. Our vision expands from its contracted state, that we might perceive a fullness in which our paths again become clear.

On this first day of the third week, we bring **Chesed** into **Tiferet**. We receive the outpouring of emotional energy from that *sefirah*, even as we bless **Chesed** in the greater "I" of **Tiferet**. We celebrate the Heart of our being.

Daily Focus:

Today I am aware of the Greater Life within me. The Light of **Tiferet** radiates from my heart space to fill me with vibrations of Compassion and Wholeness. My greater Self is blessed with Lovingkindness today. In all I meet, I witness this greater Life. My world is filled with the Spirit of Love waiting to be embraced.

Meditation for the Sixteenth Day

On this day of the journey we bring **Gevurah** into **Tiferet**, and the energies connect the heart and the left shoulder. The day is one of healing, for we take the *sefirah* of Limitation and Judgment into the *sefirah* of Compassion and Balance.

Into the Light of the Heart we bring the great Limiter, that which at once gives form to the flow of Lovingkindness from **Chesed**, limiting its expansion that it might express itself in the world. This essential paradox of **Gevurah** draws to it energies of fear and shadow. Today we shelter even that fear within the Light of Compassion.

We are not asked to deny the shadow side of our own being. We are not asked to pretend that the problematic aspects of our existence and our struggles for awareness do not exist. We are asked to bring these struggles with us, to discover ways to walk with our fears as allies, to release the power hidden within them.

We are asked to bless that which is most in need of blessing. Creation unfolds through the act of blessing that which is.

We are given all that we need in order to support the *Tikkun Olam*, the Healing Completion of Creation. The higher truth is that our experiences are absolutely fitting for each of us. When we accept them, they are no longer forced to remain as they are;

when we resist them, we keep them from changing. On this day, we particularly open to the feelings within us which are in need of blessing from our Greater Awareness.

Daily Focus:

I feel the Light grow clearer in my own heart space.
Now I bring my feelings into this Light. All aspects
of my life are illuminated with special blessing.
I awaken to a deep inner Compassion from which
I realize healing and wholeness now.

Meditation for the Seventeenth Day

In this week of **Tiferet**, we are given a Day of the Heart. We are blessed with **Tiferet** in **Tiferet**, encouraging our focus on the higher identity we call *ruach*, the non-ego identity which senses itself in all beings.

What is healed in **Tiferet**, in the space of the Heart, is the overwhelming sense of separateness with which we often experience ourselves in our world. We reach beyond that fragmentation to perceive the deeper Consciousness awakening within each of us. In this Consciousness we are always connected. That which animates all Being is One. And in **Tiferet**, we touch that One through the gift of Compassion.

Through this awareness, we understand that all human possibilities live in each of us. There is nothing which is truly foreign. When we stop throwing others from our hearts by pretending that we are better or that they are better, the possibilities for the healing of humankind can be realized. In **Tiferet**, we know intimately that any person's pain is our pain, that we are part of all humankind. In **Tiferet**, we celebrate the awakening of others and understand how their awakening supports our own.

Today we renew our dedication to healing by realizing how all human energies awaken in the One Light of this Greater Self. Indulgence of our violence makes a mockery of evolution; Compassion for our darkness opens the way to true growth.

We seek to balance the energies of light and dark, high and low, heaven and earth. From that balance, transformation emerges. In **Tiferet** we accept all selves, so we might more clearly discover the deeper Self we share. Through this Identity, we awaken to the deeper truth of our own uniqueness.

Daily Focus:

I release myself to the Light of **Tiferet** now. I allow this Light to reach outward from my heart-space to fill my entire body. I feel this Light expand beyond myself and reflect back to me from those I meet. Now all the energies of confusion and doubt within me meet in this Light. A deep inner healing flows as blessing through every cell and every level of my being. In this Light of Compassion, I am One now.

Meditation for the Eighteenth Day

Eighteen is the number of Life, since the numerical values of the letters of the Hebrew word *chai*, which means "life," add up to eighteen. This day of our journey whispers to us of deeper aspects of Life itself.

Tiferet encourages us to take joy in the steps we have already traveled in our journey from the limitations of enslavement to the responsibilities of freedom. Our current journey is built on all our journeys of the past. So we have the opportunity to reach more deeply than ever before toward our highest Visions of Self and of world.

Our journey in consciousness must be reflected as well through our acts in the world. So it is fitting that we connect today to the *sefirah* of **Netzach**, the outpouring of more physical vibration. The connection of Light is experienced between the heart and the right side of the solar plexus. The *sefirah* of vital energy is brought into **Tiferet** to be held in that place of Compassion. And **Netzach** brings **Tiferet** the vibrations through which its Wholeness and Peace may extend into the world.

Our tradition insists that spiritual awareness needs to be translated into the material world. We are the beings who have the responsibility to redeem the world in which forgetting is more popular than remembering.

We bless the energies we are given to express this Heart of Compassion in our daily lives. We allow the acceptance of that which has been to support the vision of that which can now be. We are more because of the steps we have traveled. We have learned about paths that enrich and others that impoverish. Our task is to risk the ways of expansion and evolution in our choices now.

Daily Focus:

The Light of my Heart radiates energies of celebration to all aspects of my mind, my emotions, and my body. My Spirit is illuminated by the renewed vision supported by this Joy. I am filled with blessing from all the steps I have traveled so far. I feel a new stirring of Spirit that celebrates all energies of physical vitality within me.

יהוה

Meditation for the Nineteenth Day

Into the *sefirah* of **Tiferet**, the place of the Heart, we bring **Hod**, the 'Glory' of physical perceptions and sensations. The symbolic place of **Hod** in the body is the left side of the solar plexus, so the clear channel of Light today connects that area to the heart-space.

Hod represents the form needed to hold the energetic flow from **Netzach**, allowing those energies to manifest as specific perceptions of physical sensations in the world. On the Tree of Life, we witness our continual challenge to match force and form, to balance the energies of expression with those of receptivity. One without the other cannot exist.

Yet if the force is too great for the form, the imbalance created leaves our energies spilling over aimlessly in the world. And if the form is too great for the force, we experience the hollowness of pretence.

Perfect balance, of course, is not achieved once and for all. Each new balancing leads to the next imbalance. According to the kabbalistic image, that imbalance is required for our growth. The Tree is dynamic, not static. It is a living representation of the way of evolution. And the Tree lives within each of us, as well as within every aspect of reality.

So we seek to cherish and bless each manifestation of form as well as force. Today we bring the form of physical sensation into the Compassionate Center of **Tiferet**. The Heart of our Being receives the promise of living sensations through which to express its Compassion. And all forms of sensation through which we experience ourselves in the world receive blessing, as well. Through this blessing we release resistance to our own evolution, and allow each form to become more flexible, inviting fuller energies for our next expansion.

Daily Focus:

I am the Self through whom the Eternal One thinks, feels, and speaks its Life in the world. As I become more aware of the Light of the Heart within me, I feel a deepening Compassion for all the ways in which I live in the world. As I appreciate more deeply the physical sensations I experience, the integrity of my Being unfolds with greater clarity and wisdom.

Meditation for the Twentieth Day

On this day, nearing the end of the third week of this journey, we bring **Yesod** into **Tiferet**. It is our ego identity which we bathe in the Light of Compassion today. And **Tiferet** receives the balance of Foundation within itself. The Light is focused on the central pillar of the Tree, from heart to pubic area. The promise of this day is the balancing of our lesser and Greater "I," our exclusive and our Inclusive identities.

Which "me" looks at the world at any given time determines much of what is witnessed. If it is the smaller "me," the one who is separate from all others, then issues of competition, of winning and losing, will be perceived. If it is the larger "me," the one who shares rather than competes, who *has* rather than *needs*, then a far different reality will be experienced. My Greater I realizes itself acting out all parts in the human drama, and glimpses the nature of the dance of the Whole. What is really "out there"? It depends upon who is looking.

We need both our Greater "I" and our lesser "i." The one puts us in touch with the Universe of Being; the other allows our individual biological survival on this planet, so that the Greater Awareness might touch this world.

Today we focus on blessing that lesser identity in the Light of the greater I that lives within us. All our separateness, competition, and fear are now brought into that greater Light. We do not seek to change our ego, but to more truly appreciate it. We seek to relieve it of responsibilities it cannot carry, and to support it in those it must. And we seek to provide for **Tiferet** a fit vehicle for expressing itself in the world.

Daily Focus:

The Oneness that awakens within me brings blessing to all aspects of my being. The self I bring to the world is blessed by the Self which connects me to all Being. I am grateful for the Compassion flowing always from my Greater Identity. I now share this Compassion more fully with all I meet. I am one with all that is.

יהוה

The concept of original sin - That which is our human DNA to be "cannibals". Bringing the light of compassion to our issue.

Meditation for the Twenty-first Day

We conclude each week of our meditative counting by bringing **Malchut**, the last of the *sefirot*, into the *sefirah* of the week. This week we offer up **Malchut** to **Tiferet**, that this level of Kingdom might drink fully of the Compassion that lights the Heart, and that **Tiferet** might taste the culmination of its Energy.

We focus our energies on the central pillar of the Tree. The channel of Light passes between the heart and the base of the spine. As **Malchut** and **Tiferet** meet, we enjoy a special kind of inner balance.

Malchut is the *sefirah* which symbolizes the reality in which we all live. It receives energies from all the other *sefirot*, so the vessel of **Malchut** is the most complex, and those other energies are often hidden within it. Our challenge is to discover and to honor those energies, so we might evolve more consciously.

To truly bless **Malchut** in **Tiferet** is to recognize the perfection of all that manifests. That perfection can only be perceived through the knowing that awakens at **Tiferet**. The greatest control we have over our past and our future is the attitude we take toward it, and that attitude drastically affects our present moment. To bring **Malchut** into the awareness called **Tiferet** reveals the beauty hidden within this level of reality, and supports a deep attitude of acceptance and gratitude.

Metaphysical literature often states that twenty-one days of creative meditation are necessary to alter a habit or a belief. We are now completing the first twenty-one days of this journey. We are practicing greater awareness of the energies we carry. We can trust that these meditations are taking root within our consciousness. These days of our meditative journey provide a context for Spirit to awaken within each of us.

Daily Focus:

My world is blessed this day in the Light of the Heart. The Compassion of **Tiferet** spreads through all levels of my being. I feel a new sense of balance between my inner and my outer vision. My world reflects back to me the One Who gives it Life. I cherish this Spark of Being in all I meet.

A Journey of Awakening

The Fourth Week
at Netzach:

יהוה צבאות

Perseverance of Physical Energy

I allow myself special time this week to relax into the
moment and seek the not-yet-limited vitality behind all
sensation. I become more aware of the pulsing energy
which flows through me. I am surrounded and supported
in this field of abundant Energy.

The Sefirah of the Week

Netzach, like the other two *sefirot* on the right side of the Tree of Life, represents Energy as force, which will take particular form and shape at the corresponding *sefirah* on the left side of the Tree. **Hod**, **Netzach**'s partner, provides the forms for perception and sensation; **Netzach** symbolizes the energy yearning to fill those forms.

The two sides of the Tree reflect the difference between the container and that which it contains. Form provides the vehicle through which the force can actualize. The side of force provides the 'juice' for the side of form.

We appreciate more deeply the vital energy that vibrates behind all unique perceptions, and is independent of any specific perception. The very same energy flows into the sensations we experience as positive or negative.

The Name of God

יהוה צְבָאוֹת

The Name of God at **Netzach** is pronounced *Adonai Tzeva-ot*, and written *Yod–Hay–Vav–Hay Tzeva-ot*. This Name translates as "The Eternal One of Hosts." In this context, 'hosts' refers to the sensations and perceptions which will manifest at the next *sefirah* of **Netzach**. The Name *Yod–Hay–Vav–Hay Tzeva-ot* indicates the energetic level prior to the manifestation of specific sensations.

We are invited behind the forms of our perceptions to taste the reverberation all forms carry.

This Name of God in Scripture

Adonai Tzeva-ot is with us,
the God of Jacob is our haven.

(Psalm 46:12)

The Meditative Focus

In a deepening silence, allow yourself to open to the flow of Energy, the vital force, carried within the shell of each particular sensation. Prior to definition, bask in the blessing of that outpouring. And, after you notice that definition has been made, as it always shall, move through that definition to appreciate that which is not-yet-named.

Guidelines for Intentions in the Fourth Week at Netzach

It is always a challenge to become aware of the flow of Energy before it is held in particular form. Each week that focuses on a *sefirah* on the right side of the Tree provides us this opportunity to reach behind definition to taste the living Essence prior to limitation.

Here, at **Netzach**, the flow of Awareness already contains feelings, and the influences of **Tiferet**, but those influences are not yet associated with any particular sensations or perceptions.

This week we can become more sensitive to the flow of life-energy itself. We take time to breathe it in, to experience the vibrational shifts as we inhale and exhale fully. Whatever our experience, we can notice the energy of the moment rather than the naming of that energy. As we become more aware of the naming process itself, it becomes easier to suspend that function, to taste the flow itself.

There is Life offered us this week, and we seek to open our awareness to celebrate that offering.

יהוה צבאות

Meditation for the Twenty-second Day

This is the beginning of the fourth week of our meditative journey. Our focus moves down the path of the Tree to **Netzach**, the seventh *sefirah*. **Netzach** is the place of physical vitality. The One Energy has translated through mental and emotional realms to reach this place. **Netzach** begins the realization of energies in more concrete manifestations. The work of Creation continues.

The *sefirot* are becoming more familiar. We recognize their names as well as their energies and feel them more naturally awaken as Light within our bodies. We realize the emotional as well as the physical aspects of their unfolding, and understand greater dimensions of meaning in their order and significance.

On this first day of the fourth week, we bring **Chesed** into **Netzach**, blessing the physical vibration with the free-flowing emotional energy called Lovingkindness. Our path leads us to realize and balance all the energies of the Tree as they move downward into manifestation.

We are on the right side of the Tree today, the side of force, joining the Light at the right solar plexus to the Light at the right shoulder. We awaken more fully to the incredible energies that are ours to channel and to express.

This day we seek to infuse this physical force with Lovingkindness, so it might flow more fully. We become more aware of the flow of these energies that will ultimately awaken as our physical experiences in the world.

Daily Focus:

I am a channel through whom the energies of this Universe flow. I am aware of their potential within me to bring blessing. Today my physical vitality is nourished by the spirit of Lovingkindness which is its source. I receive the fullness of this offering, that I might grow in awareness and better know the Life within me.

יהוה צבאות

4/28 - 4/29

23

Meditation for the Twenty-third Day

This is the second day of the week of **Netzach**, the week that focuses our energies at the *sefirah* of Physical Force. On this day we bring **Gevurah** into **Netzach**, experiencing the flow of Light between the left shoulder and the right side of the solar plexus.

To express our energies creatively, they need to be given form, even though that form always limits their possibilities. **Gevurah** is the great Limiter on the Tree. As such, it draws to itself names like *Judgment* and *Severity*. It is seen as the place of "evil," because of its potential for creating forms too rigid to change, forms which bring pain and suffering, as well as forms which hide an inner emptiness.

Yet **Gevurah** holds the key to all expressions of the One Energy. So we bring it into **Netzach** gently, that it might help inform our physical force in truly fruitful ways. **Gevurah** holds the secret of true receptivity, which provides the corrective for what might otherwise be the useless proliferation of form-less energies.

Often in our lives our own energies are in need of more appropriate form. We exhaust ourselves without it; our work scatters in all directions, and we produce little.

So we welcome **Gevurah** as blessing into **Netzach**, yearning to bring proper form that we might continue the great process of personal Creation. At this point in our journey, it is not possible to know exactly what forms will be appropriate for our greatest learning and our greatest sharing this year. So we allow ourselves to trust that the proper forms will emerge as we hold our vital energies in the embrace of blessing.

Daily Focus:

I support the fuller flowering of my physical energies this day. With deep and easy breathing, my body is revitalized with this vital Light. I trust that the proper forms will emerge to enable me to share my vitality in deeply creative ways. I celebrate the energies which flow through me now.

יהוה צבאות

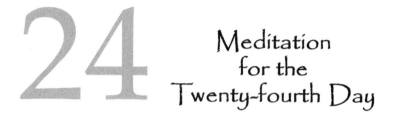

24 Meditation for the Twenty-fourth Day

The blessings of this journey expand as we become aware of the ways the One Creative Consciousness expresses as our universe. *Kabbalah* is an expanding tradition, and in our growing we add to its teachings. As we open more fully to the nature of our own Being, we are better able to participate in a greater healing and the celebration of Wholeness.

Into the weekly energy of **Netzach** we bring **Tiferet**, becoming aware of the Light connecting the right solar plexus and the heart-space. We seek to bless the expansion of Physical Vitality with the balance of Compassion at **Tiferet**. Each expansion of physical energy brings new opportunities to express Compassion more fully in the world of our experience.

We are not accidental beings in our world. We are the vehicles through whom Spirit awakens on this level of Creation, and each of us is challenged to discover our own unique ways of expressing that Spirit. Our responsibility would be greater than we could bear were it not for the profound Compassion that supports our task.

Now this Compassion grows more real because of its infusion into our own vitality. From deep within us, an inner integrity speaks more strongly of the Way which is our own. We are not asked simply to repeat the deeds and thoughts of others who have traveled their own paths of awakening. We are asked to discover the acts which are uniquely ours, the words which are waiting for us to speak.

Bringing the energies of the Heart into our daily lives encourages our own unfoldment.

Daily Focus:

Now I am infused with the Heart of all Being. From deep within me, a Greater Awareness guides the expansion of my own vitality, that it may flow with greater clarity. I cooperate with all those around me in creating a life of deeper Peace and Beauty. I am in harmony with the rhythms of all Life.

יהוה צבאות

Meditation for the Twenty-fifth Day

Today we bring the *sefirah* of **Netzach** into the week of **Netzach**. Our focus is at the right side of the solar plexus, and the *sefirah* represented there radiates especially fully now. The physical vitality that will manifest as sensation and perception are awakened within us.

Netzach this week has received the influences of expanding Lovingkindness, the Limitation of emotional form, and the balance of Compassion. All this contributes to our awareness now of Physical Energies gathering to be expressed, of all possible sensations waiting to be experienced.

There is such potential in this step of the journey. We are lifted from our weariness and infused with increased vitality. With this energy comes renewed possibility. Our task is to recognize and value these energies before form, without limitation

The evenness of yesterday's breath from **Tiferet** quickens now, as we breathe in fuller energy. There is a freer movement in the body, a recognition of greater strength than before. We open to this reflection of **Netzach** in the world within us and around us.

Old limits of Physical Energy are now released. In this realm all things are again possible. There is no end to the life-enhancing flow at **Netzach**. With curiosity and with wonder, we become aware today.

Daily Focus:

There is a great quickening of Physical Vitality within me today. Every cell of my being vibrates with the fullness of Life. A new excitement is mine as I become more aware of my world. I welcome the reverberation of this vibration everywhere. I breathe more fully the vitality of Being, and await with confidence the forms it will meet.

‎יהוה צבאות

Meditation for the Twenty-sixth Day

Hod enters the week of **Netzach** with its gifts of Perceptual Forms for the Vital Energy that has been building. The channel between the left and the right side of the solar plexus is alive with Light.

Hod is the "Glory" of physical forms manifesting as the sensations and perceptions we experience. Each sensation holds energy it receives from **Netzach**. We seek to allow that form to respond naturally to that which it receives, so that we might avoid both excessive limitation and the creation of hollow shells of pretense.

Hod allows **Netzach** to express, so each is required for Creation to take place. We are called upon to recognize the unfolding beauty of the forms with which **Netzach** is now blessed. And we witness these forms in all other beings.

There is a tension between **Netzach** and **Hod**, for in their communication true balance is difficult to achieve. In fact, each perceptual form, while containing the energy of **Netzach**, tends to close itself off from further flow. The flow of Energy yearns to be held in the form of a sensation, and then longs to be released. Energy contained too long in any shell loses its freshness, loses its connection to source.

The dynamic interplay of Energy through the *sefirot* becomes more "real" as it moves downward. Our bodies are forms in which the Energy from **Netzach** is realized, and we strive to become more available for this life-giving flow. We then open to an awareness of greater health and wholeness. We trust our cells to drink fully from the offering of **Netzach**, and to respond with new expansions and definitions of self.

Daily Focus:

I am aware of the perfection of the perceptions and sensations that now contain the vibrations of Life. I am a part of a glorious adventure of Spirit seeking to manifest Itself in continually expanding ways. With deepening confidence, I allow myself freedom to move in directions that flow from my own integrity. I celebrate all forms through which I perceive Spirit growing.

יהוה צבאות

Meditation for the Twenty-seventh Day

Today we bring **Yesod** into **Netzach**. The true manifestation of the balance of **Hod** and **Netzach** occurs at **Yesod**, the seat of ego, the place of our lesser "i," the identity with which we interact with our world. This is the Foundation from which our energies will reach out to our world.

Yesod brings this Foundation for expression into **Netzach**. From our physical sensations and perceptions comes our experience of the world. **Netzach** encourages our appreciation of that which is behind all specific forms of sensation; **Yesod** provides the avenue through which those energies will be able act in the world. No *sefirah* exists without the others, they all must interact to celebrate the great dance of Being. **Yesod** provides the balance which **Netzach** needs, and **Netzach** provides the energies that **Yesod** requires for its own fulfillment.

We feel the inner Light connect the right side of the solar plexus with the pubic area as both those areas of the body come alive with the radiance of these *sefirot*.

In **Netzach** today we recognize that aspect of ourselves which carries on the daily work of survival and of growing. **Yesod** provides a foundation within each *sefirah* even as it provides Foundation as the seat of our separate self. We can appreciate this vitality awakening within ourselves and all around us today.

Daily Focus:

My energies flow more freely now than ever before. I honor the work I do in the world, and breathe new life into my being. I know the blessing of my lesser self that carries my energies out into the world for good. I am a center of energy expressing Life this day.

יהוה צבאות

Meditation for the Twenty-eighth Day

We are four weeks into the journey, traveling both the metaphorical and the real wilderness that marks the passage from enslavement to freedom. Our slavery closes us to the Word of our Being. We journey that we might hear more clearly the Word that speaks our freedom.

This week of **Netzach** draws to a close as we connect this *sefirah* of Physical Vitality to **Malchut**, the *sefirah* of the Kingdom. Each week draws the energy of the Tree into a new balance, and each week concludes with **Malchut**, the tenth *sefirah* on the Tree of Life.

Malchut is the confusing and marvelous world of space and time in which our physical journey takes place. It is here that we have the opportunity to manifest the energies supporting our awakening, our healing, and our wholeness. Now **Malchut** infuses and is infused with the physical energy of **Netzach**. **Netzach** is offered the grounding of **Malchut**.

All the *sefirot* of the Tree of Life are waiting to be born into **Malchut**. All our meditations, our visions, and our dreams await their realization in the world of **Malchut**. Our goals seek to meet us where we already are, as we awaken more fully than ever before to the wonders of the present moment.

So **Netzach** itself is offered its own grounding in **Malchut** on this day. The Light joins **Netzach** at the right side of the solar plexus with **Malchut** at the base of the spine.

Malchut reflects the fulfillment of the Vitality of **Netzach**.

Daily Focus:

My physical energies flow freely now. I act with renewed purpose and vitality. I hold an expanding vision of a world that reflects the Wholeness and the Life that is its Source. I am one with this energy and this vision. I am a vehicle through whom the world is about to take shape.

יהוה צבאות

A Journey of Awakening

The Fifth Week
at Hod:

אלהים צבאות

The Glory of Sensation

This week I allow myself to relax into my experience,
and to release myself to explore the containers in which
my perceptions present themselves. I am able to
appreciate more fully how each sensation allows
sensory vibration to manifest. I meet the wonders of
physical sensation for their own sake now.

The Sefirah of the Week

Hod represents the forms of sensations—the images, touches, sounds, tastes, and smells that we perceive. **Hod** is on the left side of the Tree of Life, the side reflecting the forms which contain the energies offered from the right side of the Tree. Each sensory perception can be understood to be a particular container through which we experience the greater formless energy.

Physical sensation and perception allow us to know our world, and to discover ourselves within it. **Hod** brings sensory information already containing mental and emotional form. Through **Hod** we begin to truly know ourselves in the world.

The Name of God

$$\text{אֱלֹהִים צְבָאוֹת}$$

The Name of God at **Hod** is *Elohim Tzeva-ot*, which means "God of Hosts." *Elohim* reflects the aspect of the One which we meet as an "Indwelling Presence" within a world of multiplicity. *Elohim* helps us understand the truth that the One manifests as the many.

Tzeva-ot, translated "hosts," has the connotation of an "army," a group with great force. Here, the "force" is contained in the strength of each particular perception. And the *Elohim* is the Unity hidden within the apparent multiplicity of perceptual forms. Our perceptions have the strength to convince us of the reality of our world. From our perceptions we learn about ourselves in relationship to that world.

This Name of God in Scripture

Elohim Tzeva-ot, return us, illuminate Your Presence
and we shall be saved.

(Psalm 80:8)

The Meditative Focus

We move into higher levels of awareness by becoming more aware of our current experience. In **Hod** we meet the particular forms in which our perceptions present themselves, so **Hod** informs our current experience of the world.

Focus on the letters of the Name at this level, and let the sound and image of that Name provide a path for your moments of meditation. Discover the awareness supported through the vibrations of *Elohim Tzeva-ot*.

Guidelines for Intentions in the Fifth Week at Hod

Hod provides the container for **Netzach** without which **Netzach** cannot manifest. **Hod** is the sensational perception that is enlivened by **Netzach**. **Hod** is the shape of each and every perception. It is the capturing of the vibration through the senses. At this level, the vibration takes shape as that which we know sensually. Since the energies flowing to **Hod** already contain colorations from the higher *sefirot*, the forms that **Hod** provides already include the forms of thought and feeling.

There are sensations we appreciate as well as those we do not, just as there are feelings we are more comfortable with than others. Our task is to become more clearly aware of our own sensations and our own perceptions. Such open awareness invites the shifts of perception through which we learn more clearly the "secrets" those perceptions contain.

And we can become more clearly aware of the intensity of energy, the "juice" of **Netzach** which is carried by any particular sensation. We can begin to honor and explore that energy when we do not get caught up in the container. It is the acceptance of the container that allows us to move beyond it.

אלהים צבאות

Meditation for the Twenty-ninth Day

The fifth week of our process finds us at **Hod**, the space called Glory, the place of form which receives the vibrational force from **Netzach**. **Hod** is experienced at the left side of the solar plexus, on the left side of the Tree of Life. **Hod** represents physical form, expressing as our sensations and perceptions, and so is the seat of the special delights and special dilemmas we experience in our world.

We get so caught up in our perceptions and our sensations. Nothing supports our tendency to judge quite as naturally. We are part of a society which continually evaluates us according to our perceived size and shape. Who among us is free from such self-evaluation? And, in this world of form, how often do we experience ourselves as either "too much" or "too little," rather than "just right"?

Yet without such comparisons, we cannot experience our world. At each level of form on the Tree, the issues are the same. So we seek to discover ways to utilize our limits in the service of growth and evolution.

Today we bring **Chesed** into **Hod**. The channel of light connects the left side of our solar plexus to our right shoulder. We bring the *sefirah* of Lovingkindness into the *sefirah* of

Perceptual Form. And in this connection we seek to bless **Hod** with the energies which can inspire finer and more complete forms.

With **Chesed** in **Hod**, we open ourselves to reflect the deep Lovingkindness that provides profoundly healing energies. We seek to better perceive reflections of that Lovingkindness today. We seek to sense the presence of that freely-flowing source of Life.

Daily Focus:

My senses provide an embodiment of Spirit. The blessing of Lovingkindness supports me in my body and quiets my sense of physical limitation. I become more aware of the Energy I carry through every cell of my body. I breathe the freshness of **Chesed**, that it might influence all my thoughts, my feelings, and my perceptions. I cherish my experiences through which I discover my connections to others and to my world.

אלהים צבאות

Meditation for the Thirtieth Day

This is the week of **Hod**, the "Glory" of Physical Form met through our sensations and our perceptions. Into **Hod** we bring **Gevurah**, the Severity of Emotional Limitation. We focus our energies on the left side of the Tree, experiencing the connection as a channel of light between the left solar plexus and the left shoulder.

This is a day for consolidating our energies, for appreciating the forms into which they are cast. We are offered precious moments to consider the shape of the emotions which we discover associated with our sensations and perceptions. We are challenged to care tenderly for our physical selves, and to become more aware than ever of our power to translate energies of wholeness into the world of being.

The world of forms is so confusing to us. Too often, we fail to contain our powerful emotions in feelings that support growth, and instead let these energies express in feelings that lead us astray. So we strive more consciously to choose the limits, that we may appreciate more fully the multitude of feelings we experience. To walk in ways of holiness requires an expanding and accepting awareness.

Our meditations for this day focus on the valuations we place on our sensations, on our experiences in the world. We would shape ourselves into vehicles of healing, that we might see beyond the transient impressions of sensation and physical form.

Daily Focus:

I am a vehicle through whom Universal Energies flow. Now these forces find perfect form to express themselves for healing in my world. I bless the sensations through which I know my body and my world. My vision expands that I might bless the evolving dimensions of my physical experience in the world.

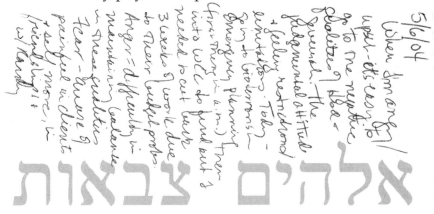

אלהים צבאות

Meditation for the Thirty-first Day

We bring the energies of **Tiferet**, Beauty and Compassion, into our weekly *sefirah* of **Hod** today. Into the space of Physical Sensation we bring the blessings of the Heart, that Compassion might soothe the journey of the body in ordinary time and space.

The connection of Light is between the left side of the solar plexus and the heart-space. In our struggle to discover through ordinary life the purpose and meaning that whispers from our Source, **Tiferet** brings ever greater clarity and Light.

We envision our physical being responding to the rhythms of the Universe with renewed health and vitality. We strive to express in all ways that which we know to be supportive of ourselves and of others.

In the midst of this ancient/new wilderness, where there is so much confusion and doubt, despair and pain, we can still choose to acknowledge the vision of wholeness. We insist that our lives have meaning, that our actions and our words can indeed elicit responses far beyond our limited selves' ability to conceive.

With the Heart of Compassion glowing strongly within all our sensations, we reach out more surely into the world around us. We would translate this Compassion through every cell of our beings. We would perceive it reflected back to us from all we touch. Nothing is truly separate from the Source of all Life we share.

Daily Focus:

I walk this planet now with a new sense of inner balance. The Compassion that awakens in the Heart of my being radiates through my sensory awareness. I know that this deeper Beauty of Being expresses through me. Through the sensations I experience I discover this Compassion revealed. Creation expands through me now.

צבאות אלהים

 Meditation
for the
Thirty-second Day

On this day of our meditative journey, we bring **Netzach** into the weekly *sefirah* of **Hod**. There is a meeting of Physical Vitality in the *sefirah* of Physical Sensation and Perception. The Light connects left and right sides of the solar plexus, and we feel grounded and blessed in our physical beings.

We have traveled far already on this journey, and we welcome these energies that allow us to proceed yet further. We begin to know more clearly the possibilities that reside in our awareness of physical forms. Our bodies allow us to actualize the Spirit for Whom we are messengers in the world.

Hod now receives from **Netzach** the outpouring of energy with which it can inform itself most effectively. Without these energies, we are in danger of living as shells devoid of substance. How often we get caught up in a specific perception, forgetting that the true beauty and meaning comes from appreciating the Vitality it contains.

We seek to open our cells on this day to receive the vibration that fills our perceptions with Life, that energy which allows us to grow and to express in positive ways. Our world is in great need of positive perceptions of this Universal Energy.

In our week of **Hod**, we seek the essential mystery behind the physical appearance of this Universe. We seek to know the fuller expression of the One Who infuses all form. Without this One, no form could be. Without the form of **Hod**, we could not know the expression of this One.

Daily Focus:

I trust now that there is within me a deep meeting of energy and form. With every sensation, I experience the holiness of Spirit in the world. Deeper meaning and greater purpose flow through all my perceptions. I am a channel for the One Life that celebrates all Creation with Blessing.

אלהים צבאות

Meditation for the Thirty-third Day

The thirty-third day of the traditional counting of the *Omer* is called *Lag B'Omer*, named by the acronym formed by the two Hebrew letters that indicate the number thirty-three. This is a special day of celebration during the actual Omer period, a day of great Light and rejoicing. According to some mystics, the number thirty-three is the highest spiritual number in the progression of the significant numbers eleven and twenty-two.

In this week of **Hod**, the *sefirah* called "Glory," this is the day of **Hod** in **Hod**. The Light radiates fully at the left side of the solar plexus. This eighth *sefirah* symbolizes the physical sensations through which we perceive and understand our world, so this is a day to celebrate the form through which Spirit manifests in our world. Form always limits the fullness of Spirit, yet at the same time allows it to operate as an expression of Creation. So this is a day of celebrating the Creation that expresses through the forms in which we live, particularly focusing on the form of our sensations.

We are such amazing beings. We can know forms which constrict the energies available to us, and rob the universe of that which we might give it. And we can know forms far too great for the energy, and so experience greater and greater levels of frustration. **Hod** holds the possibility of forms which most joyfully and appropriately contain the energy they hold, and it is this possibility that we celebrate today.

Traditionally, this is a day to celebrate the world of nature, connecting more concretely with our physical world. When we welcome perceptions of the natural world, there is often an opening, a relaxing of the usual sensations we habitually entertain. This is a day for appreciating such Glory.

Daily Focus:

I am a perfect vehicle for experiencing and expressing the One Spirit manifesting as this world. Through me, Spirit flows Its Life of joy and celebration. The mental, emotional, and perceptual forms of my life expand to reflect fuller dimensions of healing and wholeness now. I celebrate the One I preceive.

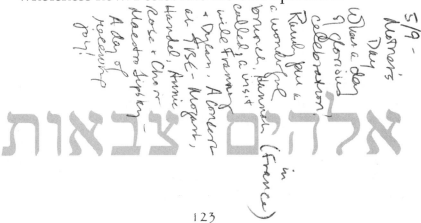

Meditation for the Thirty-fourth Day

A day of rejoicing draws to a close, and we are back on our journey, almost to the end of the fifth week. If we are to look back now, our stepping out from old enslavement is further back than we thought. Much has happened. We are moving more deeply into the greater adventure of our Being.

This thirty-fourth day of our journey brings **Yesod** into **Hod**. Into the sefirah expressing sensation and perception, we bring the *sefirah* of our individual identity. **Yesod** carries the energies of the ego-self, with which we must continually interact in the world.

The channel of Light we experience today links the left side of the solar plexus to the genital area. We are moving further toward our goal of manifesting more clarity and blessing in the physical world.

Yesod is so in need of the Glory of Form which **Hod** can express. And **Hod**, in turn, needs the vehicle through which that form can act in the world of being. Each *sefirah* balances the others. None can manifest alone. None is less significant than any other in the process of Creation. Each aspect of our being is crucial and precious, just as each of us is crucial and precious in our world.

Personal responsibility awakens at **Yesod**. So today we bring that sense of responsibility into the form at **Hod**. Perception must find its observer through whom it can be known in the world. Our perceptions help shape the very nature of our identity, since the creation we experience is a transaction between the observer and that which is observed. **Hod** informs **Yesod** with its sensations, and **Yesod** bases its identity upon the nature of its perceptions.

Daily Focus:

Today I become more sensitive to the ways in which my sensations and perceptions influence my identity. Behind every particular sensation is a freely flowing vital energy; every perception is simply one container through which that energy can be experienced. I am always more than my perceptions. I am a channel for the energies of a Universe.

אלהים צבאות

Meditation for the Thirty-fifth Day

The week at **Hod** completes itself by welcoming the tenth *sefirah* of **Malchut**. With the *sefirah* called Kingdom, the meditative cycle is grounded each week. We experience the connection of Light today as a channel between the left side of the solar plexus and the base of the spine.

The energy of the Tree flows to each *sefirah* and allows that *sefirah* to serve the Whole. Each *sefirah* is fed by what it receives, and then contributes its own aspect, allowing Creation to unfold as it does. In **Malchut**, the energy of all the *sefirot* actualize in the world in which we live.

During this meditative process, we are energetically balancing the lower seven *sefirot* of the Kabbalistic Tree of Life. In so doing, we create an environment of balanced receptivity. The culmination of this journey is the openness for Revelation at a moment called Sinai. We prepare what we can, and trust that the upper three *sefirot* will meet us in that Moment. At Sinai, our awareness of the Tree is Whole. That is the nature, always, of authentic Revelation.

As we complete this week, we appreciate more than ever the functioning of **Hod**, the *sefirah* of perception and sensation, which lends stability and sense to our physical experience. We seek this stability through all the steps we take on our journey in the wilderness this year.

Of course, that which holds the key to our growth can also serve to enslave us. Such is the Way of our Universe. So we look around us now with fuller awareness. Our goal is to sense the rightness of all we see, of all we hear, of all we experience. We rejoice that we are given the realities of the sensations with which we can know our path toward healing and wholeness, and we seek to celebrate the One who meets us through all sensation.

Daily Focus:

I am a being through whom the Universal Consciousness walks this planet. Through my physical form, I have precious opportunities to experience and express the blessings of Love, Compassion, and Vitality. I welcome all my sensations and learn to sense the Oneness hidden within them.

אלהים צבאות

A Journey of Awakening

The Sixth Week
at Yesod:

שדי אל חי

Center and Foundation

This week I honor the one at the center of my thoughts, my feelings, and my perceptions. I allow myself to appreciate this center of my being by remaining open to the moment. I watch my judgments, my feelings, and my sensations. I welcome them from the center of my individual self.

The Sefirah of the Week

Yesod represents the "Foundation" of our separate sense of self. It is the self-awareness that we call "ego." This is the place of our *nefesh*, the level of soul which is associated with the body. At **Yesod,** we know the "I" of the storm, the identity from which we can most effectively act in the world.

Yesod is also the *sefirah* of generation, represented on the body by the genitals. The ego identity is the body identity, and the body identity is deeply connected to our sexuality. It is important to appreciate how an energy which supports life can also be turned against itself. As we move down the Tree, and the energies become more dense, there is greater need for fuller awareness.

The Names of God

אֵל חַי   שַׁדַּי

The kabbalistic tradition assigns two Names of God at **Yesod**: *Shaddai* and *El Chai*. *Shaddai* ("The Almighty") is a Name reflecting the Power of God, and it is inscribed on the outside of the *mezuzah* scroll, and often on the outside front of the *mezuzah* itself. The *mezuzah* is a small cylindrical container holding a handwritten parchment upon which several central verses from the Torah are inscribed. It is placed on the right side of a doorway (as one enters a home or a room). So *Shaddai* is a Name of protection and of identification. *El Chai* ("The Living God" or "The

God of Life") draws our awareness to the channeling of Life energy through the *sefirah* of **Yesod**. Remember that when "ch" appears as a transliteration of Hebrew, it is pronounced as a guttural "kh" sound.

While we tend to denigrate the significance of our ego identity, this *sefirah* encourages a greater appreciation for the possibilities for which our separate self exists. The ego is a vehicle through which more profound spiritual consciousness can connect to the manifest world. We each serve as a channel for the Life and for the Power of God. So this week we focus on the promise contained within our individual identities.

These Names of God in Scripture

Let *El Shaddai* bless you.

(Genesis 28:3)

My soul thirsts for *El Chai*.

(Psalm 42:3)

The Meditative Focus

During your meditations this week, become more aware of the self behind your experience. Who is the one receiving your thoughts, feelings, and sensations? Use all your experiences this week to learn more about the central identity who has them.

Take **Shaddai** and **El Chai** as the sounds and the letter-images upon which you focus this week. As you do so, what do you experience? Explore these two names and the energies they carry.

Guidelines for Intentions in the Sixth Week at Yesod

Yesod is the Foundation from which **Malchut**, the manifestation, will flow. Psychologically, **Yesod** is the place of the individual identity called the ego. At **Yesod**, the essential identity needed for ensuring the individual biological survival of the organism is forged. Although the ego is often denigrated, it is not "bad." Ego is required, and the stronger the ego, the better. It is the weak ego that seeks to usurp for itself power beyond its capabilities, and then to attempt to be what it cannot by trying to control others and the world.

That **Yesod** is identified with sexuality is appropriate, for much of our individual identity is rooted there. Sexuality offers a clear reflection of the dilemma of our separate selves. We experience incompleteness and seek, as it were, our "other half" with which to know an elusive completeness. Of course, that "other half" outside us is a reflection of the "other half" hidden within us. When the ego discovers its own integrity, its own essential wholeness, then it can express more clearly, and open to a greater identity within which the ego itself is held with great Compassion.

This week we seek more clearly to know, appreciate, and honor the shape of our separate self. The model of the Tree of Life supports our deeper understanding of the way mental, emotional, and perceptual forms create our sense of self. We seek greater awareness, not to blame, but to better understand and appreciate the nature of our being. Our intention is to manifest the energies we discover within ourselves in more loving and more healing ways.

שדי אל חי

Meditation for the Thirty-sixth Day

This week we focus our attention at **Yesod**, the place where we awaken as individualized beings in the world, as our ego-selves. The One Being individualizes Itself in order to express on this level of existence. The cost of individualization is always the awareness of separation.

Into this space that knows separateness we bring **Chesed**, with its energy of Lovingkindness, as we begin the sixth week of this meditative process. We imagine the inner connection as a channel of light between the genital area and the right shoulder.

Yesod is the center identified with sexuality because that is symbolic of one of the most basic needs of our biological selves. Ego is that identity with which we sustain ourselves as individual biological entities in the world. Our challenge is to support the growth of ego without expecting it to take on tasks and responsibilities which are beyond its abilities.

It is through our ego-self that we relate to one another, and cooperate in the process we call Creation. Ego is a channel through whom higher energies can reach into ordinary reality. So we strive to honor this aspect of our identity, to strengthen it, and to support other egos around us.

But our body-self often seeks to claim the universe as its own, to see itself as the center of all existence. This posture of egocentricity leads always to great personal and global pain. Extreme self-involvement shuts out others and makes a mockery of the spiritual path. So we bring **Chesed**, Lovingkindness, into **Yesod** to support the more loving and fluid expression of this identity.

Daily Focus:

I realize more fully than ever before the worth of my separate self. I feel the blessings of Lovingkindness awaken now within me, and know that there are fuller ways in which I can express this energy in my world. I am grateful for this opportunity to honor the preciousness of the individual self within me and within all I meet.

 שדי אל חי

Meditation for the Thirty-seventh Day

The first step in this week of **Yesod** infused this ninth *sefirah* with the energies of **Chesed**. Now it is time to limit Lovingkindness with **Gevurah**, the *sefirah* of Emotional Boundaries. The Acceptance and Lovingkindness we carry must have proper form if it is to express meaningfully in our world. On this day we feel the channel of Light between the genital area and the left shoulder.

Honoring the ego, the identity which awakens at **Yesod**, is one of our greatest challenges. From the lesser "i," our more limited point of view, we experience a constant parade of judgments and comparisons with which we separate ourselves from ourselves, from others, and from our world. Yet **Gevurah**, that first sefirah of separation, reminds us of the necessity of such separations. This is the way of Creation itself. We are challenged to remember that even our judgments and comparisons can be for blessing when they help orient us in our world, when they teach us to better use ourselves as vehicles of Divine Purpose.

The ego functions as an environment that reflects the polarities awakening at **Gevurah**. Just as **Gevurah** allows fuller energies to manifest, so Yesod becomes the necessary vehicle for walking holiness into our world. We are reminded that all aspects of our being proclaim the glory of the One we are, so we do not seek to rid ourselves of shadow, but to utilize its energies in the service of our evolution.

It is too easy to collapse into the darkness we meet in our shadow self. Our goal, instead, is to appreciate even those aspects of ourselves that carry forgetfulness, fear, insecurity, and inadequacy. By re-owning the rejected aspects of our ego, we are finally able to make allies of our fears and journey more meaningfully into the wilderness entrusted to us.

Daily Focus:

I become aware of deeper aspects of my being today. There is light as well as shadow within me, and I honor both as I journey toward my fuller awakening. I welcome the new forms I discover through which I can express my uniqueness in the world. A deep trust in all aspects of my being awakens now.

שדי אל חי

Meditation
for the
Thirty-eighth Day

Today **Tiferet** is brought into the weekly *sefirah* of **Yesod**. The connection of Light flows between the genital area and the heart-space, as the blessing of the Heart illuminates our ego identity. We welcome that blessing into the part of ourselves most in need of such Light.

We are manifestations of the One Source of all Life. Yet it is through the separate self that we must carry this Source into the world. The separate ego self serves as a messenger for that which it cannot contain within itself.

According to a kabbalistic metaphor, we are given the task of redeeming the sparks of the One Light which have become encased in *kelipot*, in the husks of material reality. In order to do so, we must enter that world in which that Light is hidden. But the husks are so convincing! How easy it is to forget the One Who lives within them.

Our separate self is itself one such *kelipah*. It is a shell that hides the Indwelling Presence called *Shechinah*. We cover that inner Identity with shadows of fear, of worry, of judgment and comparison. We dress ourselves in the "not-yet's" and the "almost's" and the "not-good-enough's" that spring up endlessly within our minds.

We are the beings on this level of reality who are given the responsibility of remembering Who we are. When we sink into despair, we draw our shells more firmly about us. When we open to the joys of existence, our shells thin, and we are better able to awaken to our fuller Identity. **Tiferet** teaches the deep acceptance of our individual selves that is itself the path of such remembering.

Tiferet, the *sefirah* of our Greater Self, is given us this day for additional focus. When we allow ourselves to open to the gentle touch of that deep Compassion, we are led from places of despair back into the Light of our Being.

Daily Focus:

I breathe deeply and release the tensions with which I have surrounded myself. I become aware of the deeper influences of Compassion that awaken within me. This Light flows through me now as a peaceful healing radiance. I rest in the glow of the Presence within.

Meditation for the Thirty-ninth Day

Into this week of **Yesod**, the Foundation of our being in the world, today we bring **Netzach**, the reverberation of Physical Vibration. The channel of Light connects the pubic area and the right solar plexus of the body.

We allow our lesser self to be revitalized by **Netzach**, that it might have the energy required to authentically express its uniqueness in the world.

The ego, our sense of separate self, is the precious identity in which we usually live. Our task is to create an ego able not only to support our own emerging self, but also to support those around us.

We seek to avoid the trap of simply comparing ourselves to some external model, and instead reach deeply inside to discover our own truths. It takes great courage to bring ourselves into the open. At the same time, we need to be mindful of the search of others. We are not meant to simply replicate one another, but to co-exist and cooperate with honesty and with caring.

This courage flows from **Netzach** now. Our energies are renewed and deepened. We allow ourselves to feel this revitalization through every cell of our bodies. The exhaustion of our journey lifts. There is new strength to move ahead.

So we particularly honor the Vitality which allows us to create a self worthy of the Self Who lives through us. Today gives us space to appreciate the fuller strength of our individual being.

Daily Focus:

Today I am filled with new vitality and Spirit. A deep self-acceptance supports a new flowering of my awareness now. I am at peace with my world.

אל חי   שדי

Meditation for the Fortieth Day

There is something special about the number forty—it is a symbol of a radical change in awareness. It rained forty days and nights during Noah's time, Moses was alone atop the Mountain twice for forty days, and we wandered the wilderness for forty years. In Jewish mystical tradition, there are four worlds. In each of the worlds there is a Tree of Life with ten *sefirot*, and four Trees yield forty *sefirot*.

Traditionally we are cautioned against studying kabbalah before the age of forty. This is not a measure of time as much as a measure of awareness. We are to be well-grounded before such study can be of true meaning.

Perhaps the forty days we have already spent on our journey this year are symbolic of such preparation. Perhaps we are more ready now to receive that which awaits us at Sinai.

The journey is never an easy one. In the true wilderness, we will be met by the crucial issues of our lives. And we will also meet the deeper goals which unfold with each step. The wilderness is the place of transforming our resistances into blessings.

On this fortieth day, in the week of **Yesod**, we welcome the *sefirah* of **Hod**, the Glory of sensations and perceptions. We wish to realize those forms of sensation within ourselves which can support the expression of the Being Who dwells within us. The channel of Light connects the pubic area and the left side of the solar plexus. The receptive side of the Tree strengthens our ego self now.

Hod is the *sefirah* of the perception of physical beauty. This is not only a superficial beauty, but the inner beauty we experience as holiness. It is this deep beauty, in which form expands more fully to celebrate the Energy offered it, that we celebrate this day.

Daily Focus:

There is profound beauty which awakens within me now. I feel the blessing of this form as renewed confidence. Fuller abilities to realize my unique path unfold for me now. I express this realization through every thought and every action in my life.

Meditation for the Forty-first Day

This day focuses on **Yesod**; it is **Yesod** in **Yesod**. Our focus is on that *sefirah* which symbolizes the energies of our lesser self, our ego consciousness, our separate sense of self. The Light is centered in the genital area. This is the energetic center of sexuality, which is central to our ego self. It is central to the ego's task of individual biological survival.

Our challenge is to keep the ego open to those energies which flow from less separate aspects of Self, for then we can manifest the fuller truth of our being. We are separate and at the same time One. We are the One manifesting as the many.

We are animal, yet we are more. Our minds awaken with the vision of the Whole. Our hearts sing with the harmony of the Universe. We would translate the image and the song into the material world of our physical senses. We are the beings who have the opportunity of remembering Who we are.

We are not asked to kill ego, but to actualize through it our fuller Being. Our Way is not to deny the urges of our lesser "i," but to utilize those urges in the service of healing and wholeness.

It is to this that we are called. It is for this that our world needs us. We strengthen our separate self with all the energies available to us now. We bless the opportunity we are given to channel our True Being into specific thoughts, feelings, and actions bringing healing into our world. We are aware of the strengths now of our individual identity.

Daily Focus:

My separate self vibrates with Life. Through me, the Universe thinks, feels, and speaks. Through me, the One touches the material world with the gifts of Spirit. The blessings I carry reveal themselves now. I celebrate my individual self that carries holiness into the everyday world.

חי אל שׁדי

Meditation for the Forty-second Day

We experience our journey unfolding wherever we choose to walk. That which was so distant grows more near. We are six weeks out from our place of enslavement. And we are on our way to our place of awakening.

This has been our week at **Yesod**, focusing on the energies of the ego, of our lesser self. On this final day of this week, we bring **Malchut**, the *sefirah* representing the Kingdom, into **Yesod**. The channel of Light connects the lower *sefirot* on the central pillar of the Tree of Life, the pubic area and the base of the spine.

Malchut is the final *sefirah*, into which all the energies moving through the Tree of Life finally flow. The energies of each *sefirah* are no longer quite so distinct, but they are waiting to be discovered within **Malchut**.

Malchut is where all this happens. It is the place within which we are given the opportunity to awaken. It is the place of enslavement, and it is the place of freedom. This is the wonderful Kingdom of Possibility.

Malchut is the *sefirah* which grounds all those above it. In electrical systems, without a suitable and stable "ground," the current cannot flow fully and clearly. So it is with our model of

the Tree of Life. We need a stable grounding to allow energies
on the entire Tree to flow freely and with purpose.

Malchut provides the environment in which we can stand.
Malchut today brings that reality into **Yesod**, the Foundation of
our sense of separate self.

Daily Focus:

I feel the energies of a Universe flow through me now.
I am a channel through whom heaven and earth meet.
My journey grows clearer as I celebrate the blessings
of my separate self. I act to translate these blessings
to all those around me.

A Journey of Awakening

The Seventh Week
at Malchut:

אדני

Actualization

I allow moments of quiet this week to explore more fully
my current experience in the world. Without trying to
change anything, I allow myself to explore where I am
now in the life I am living. I open to the fullness of Life
that meets me now.

The Sefirah of the Week

Malchut represents the "kingdom" in which we live, and is the level of the Tree which receives from all others. Energies from the higher *sefirot* manifest here, but they are hidden. **Malchut** is the *sefirah* in which we can lose ourselves, but it is also the place in which we must find ourselves.

Malchut encourages us to become more open to the wonders of the kingdom in which we are living right now. So we seek to quiet ourselves in order to pay more exquisite attention to the myriad of impulses—physical, emotional, and mental— with which each moment is filled. And in this quiet space of expanding awareness, we can release ourselves more fully to our experience, letting go of the breath and letting go of the resistance. Everything is simply as it is right now.

Through this meditative expansion of attention, we seek to become aware of the energies of each of the other *sefirot* as they are reflected in **Malchut**. We bind ourselves and our universe together through our awakening in each absolutely unique and full moment.

Malchut can be a place of stuckness or a place of possibility. The more we are willing simply to honor our experience, to explore it without resistance, the more able we are to discover the possibilities which are otherwise hidden from us.

The Name of God

אֲדֹנָי

Adonai is the Name associated with **Malchut**. *Adonai* literally means "Lord," and is the word we read instead of the unspeakable Name of Four Letters. Here, *Adonai* is spelled as it sounds. On this level of **Malchut**, we are asked to appreciate the word "Lord" itself, since there is limited ability to realize more inclusive levels of identity.

At **Malchut**, it is necessary to awaken to levels which are hidden, so even the Name of God reflects a place of possible alienation. Yet it may be through this very alienation and limitation that we can most directly awaken to the deeper whispers moving through this dimension of reality.

This Name of God in Scripture

Adonai, open my lips, that my mouth may declare Thy glory.

(Daily Prayerbook)

The Meditative Focus

During your meditations this week, become more aware of your surroundings. In moments of quiet, allow yourself to notice more of what is going on both outside as well as inside. Begin to release the resistance to aspects of your world which you are finding difficult to notice. Let be what is.

Take *Adonai* as your focus. Explore the sound, the letters, and the meaning of that Name.

Guidelines for Intentions in the Seventh Week at Malchut

We have focused on the flow of energies on the Tree, the unfolding of Creation, and we now arrive at the most complex of manifestations—the world in which we live. This is **Malchut**, the Kingdom, which receives from all of the other *sefirot*. This is the place in which we can most easily be lost. And, paradoxically, it is as well the place in which we can most easily be found.

The shape of our **Malchut**, the shape of our current reality, reflects the energies that make it up, so we can understand a great deal from a clearer examination of our world. As always, allowing ourselves to experience with deeper compassion opens the gateways to greater awareness. It is our resistance that keeps us locked up. Resistance to a place of stuckness enhances that very stuckness.

Malchut is the place in which we can create opportunities for awakening. It is here we prepare ourselves to stand at Sinai—the place of greater hearing. And so we strive to understand more fully the nature of this current reality.

In **Malchut** we can become lost even to ourselves. When we identify with the particulars of **Malchut**, we forget the self beyond those identifications. We identify with power, with position, with person, with possession, with fame, and with money. The list is endless. Yet it is through this very process of identification that we can better discover ourselves. To honor where we are, and then to move behind how we are currently experiencing ourselves and our world, allows us to expand the potentials of our **Malchut**. For this Kingdom is the place in which the Greater Being seeks us now.

Meditation for the Forty-third Day

We now begin the final week of this process. It is the week of **Malchut**, the tenth *sefirah*. **Malchut** is the Kingdom, representing this world in which all the energies of the Tree of Life converge and manifest. According to some kabbalistic formulations, this is the *sefirah* of *Shechinah*, the Indwelling Presence, the feminine aspect of God's Oneness. This is the material world in which the spiritual awaits realization.

Malchut is the place in which we play out our earthly drama. We are born into this Kingdom much as we are born into our bodies. Our purpose here is to realize Who we are, that we might contribute to the completion of creation on this realm.

Into **Malchut** we bring **Chesed** today. We bring blessing from the place of Lovingkindness into the lower *sefirah* which is so in need of that Love. The Light today connects the base of the spine and the right shoulder.

In **Malchut** there is so much confusion. It is so difficult to tell exactly what is going on. The days of this week attain special importance as we seek to perceive the manifestation of higher energies in this material world. In some ways, **Malchut** is the most crucial *sefirah*, since it is the "place" we live. **Malchut** provides the ground for Creation to manifest. **Malchut** is the *sefirah* where the Presence can be met.

We are challenged to discover the Light within a world of light and shadow. So we begin this week in **Malchut** with Lovingkindness.

Daily Focus:

Lovingkindness infuses my world now. Its gentle Radiance illuminates all levels of my universe. Through that Light, I celebrate all Life about me. My world is blessed with Love.

אדני

Meditation for the Forty-fourth Day

The Mystery unfolds for us where we are, and our living space is called **Malchut**, the Kingdom. This is the final week of our meditative journey, and we focus on the place in which we dwell. Here we find the questions that spur our journey; here we find the answers hidden where we would least expect them.

On this level of reality, we are to discover traces of the energies that carry deeper meaning and purpose. Today we bring **Gevurah** into **Malchut**, to focus on the energies from that *sefirah* that infuse our world. The channel of Light connects the base of the spine to the left shoulder. We seek to construct forms which allow us to utilize the emotional energies of our world in creative and healing ways. We seek to discover the shape of our feelings in ways expressive of the Love we can carry.

Gevurah provides the limits to the free and formless expression from **Chesed**. Our world is a world of limits, a world of boundaries and barriers. We are called upon to appreciate at deeper levels the blessing which flows from these very limits. A boundary permits the definition which allows us to function in the world. Perhaps it is only through such limitation that we can truly attain the awareness that expands beyond all limits. This is the promise of **Gevurah** in **Malchut**.

Our feelings are always shifting. We live in a dynamic universe of emotion. We cannot hold our positive feelings for any great length of time, yet it seems we can more easily maintain our negative feelings. We can always find something wrong somewhere. Our task is to allow both positive and negative feelings, that we might truly learn the lessons of creation and of growth.

Daily Focus:

I honor all the feelings which flow through me now. I become aware of the constant shifting of energies within me, and no longer struggle to hide what I feel. I have a deep trust in the creative rhythm of my inner life. I become more aware of the shape of my feelings than ever before.

Meditation for the Forty-fifth Day

Into the weekly *sefirah* of **Malchut** we bring **Tiferet**, the *sefirah* of Beauty and of Balance. **Tiferet** is the space of our Greater Self, the "I" with which we perceive our connections to all Life. Within this identity our awareness expands, and we are able to know the Compassion which brings blessing to all it experiences. The channel of Light connects the base of the spine to the space of the heart.

Our world, **Malchut**, is yearning for these blessings, and it is our responsibility to express them here. In the up-and-down, high-and-low fluctuations at **Malchut**, we ride the roller coaster of feelings. We touch great heights of joy and plunge into lows that often seem deepest when our joys have been the highest. We seek that Compassion which can help us see beyond the moments of darkness to know the larger rhythms of which we are a part.

Tiferet brings the Heart into this world. **Tiferet** carries the Light that can help us remember that there is more, that we are more. **Tiferet** carries the awakening of Deep Acceptance—the acceptance of the here and now that can lead us beyond any apparent impasse.

Since **Malchut** is our Kingdom, we are now working with the actual experiences in our own lives. So we would do well to consider our own spaces of darkness, and dare to realize the Light that awaits us right here where we are now. This Heart energy expands our vision to allow us to see new possibilities. We are called upon to dream the dreams of growing, particularly at moments when growth seems so impossible.

Daily Focus:

Beyond the confusion and the doubts which I experience, there is an inner Light waiting to be perceived. From that Light I discover the gentle flow of Compassion available to me now. I hear the whispers of blessing behind all the events of my life.

46
Meditation for the Forty-sixth Day

Into our week of **Malchut** today we bring **Netzach**, the *sefirah* of Physical Vitality. The channel of Light extends between the base of the spine and the right side of the solar plexus.

Malchut contains such a confusing array of energies, and dealing with our world tends to deplete those energies. **Netzach** is the *sefirah* that infuses our world now with the Physical Endurance we need to continue on the final steps of our journey this year.

Netzach is the corrective to the energy drain we experience both personally and globally. It is the breath, flowing freely and fully, revitalizing the cells of the body of this Kingdom.

Netzach manifests as well in Physical Vibrations that serve to further confuse us in this realm. We need that which **Netzach** offers us, and need to learn to appreciate this energy for its own sake beyond any of the forms in which it appears.

Our task on this day is to discover and honor these energies wherever we find them. We are challenged to affirm those forces even when they frighten us with their intensity. Then we can utilize them most effectively, and disperse the clouds of physical depression which we so often experience.

Daily Focus:

I open myself to the energies that now flow into my world, knowing that they revitalize all that is. I rejoice as I awaken to the fuller aspects of my Being. A new vitality is mine now, supporting my fuller sharing with my world.

Meditation for the Forty-seventh Day

The final days of our journey are at hand. The conclusion of a journey holds such different energies than those of the beginning.

We are walking deeper into the world of **Malchut**, the Kingdom which receives all energies flowing downward on the Tree of Life. Today we focus on **Hod** in **Malchut**, honoring the Physical Containers we know through our senses and perceptions. The channel of Light connects the base of the spine with the left side of the solar plexus.

In our preparations for the Meeting at Sinai, we seek to balance the polarities of force and form on the Tree of Life and in ourselves. Our task is not to deny either side, but to learn to honor both. In each are excesses and deficits that only the other can balance.

Hod symbolizes Perceptual Form that is able to contain and express the Physical Vibrations at **Netzach**. Only **Hod** can provide creative and healing forms to channel those energies. All energetic expression craves the appropriate limitations of form in order to actualize in ways supportive of creative evolution.

In **Malchut** we need to remember that balance is possible, that all the many facets of reality are aspects of the One, that through our own consciousness we can realize the beauty and the glory of each living being.

So we hold to the preciousness of **Hod** on this day. We celebrate the Forms through which we experience the dramas of our days. We honor appearances that we might better see beyond them.

Daily Focus:

I trust my journey more fully now than ever before. I am aware that all the forms of my experience are holding higher energies. I become ever more available to the deeper realities of my world.

Meditation for the Forty-eighth Day

We are meeting the energies of the *sefirot* as they flow into **Malchut**, the *sefirah* of this final week of this 49-day journey. Into **Malchut**, this Kingdom, we bring **Yesod**, the place of our ego. **Yesod** is the Foundation of our lesser "i" with which we interact with each other and with our world. The channel of Light is experienced between the base of the spine and the genital area.

It is all too possible to exist at **Malchut** losing awareness of **Yesod**, forgetting our fuller ego-self. The ego itself is an awakening of self-consciousness, without which we live with no perception of meaning and purpose beyond the identification with role, person, or pattern in **Malchut**.

Ego is the link between our Higher Self and this world. With its light and its shadow, its joy and its sorrow, its failures and its accomplishments, our ego allows to us stand firm in the world. It is our vehicle for orienting thought, feeling, and action toward greater purpose.

With all its struggles, all its difficulties, our lesser self carries its own wisdom and power into the world of **Malchut**. It allows us our unique point of view, through which we can understand and operate in the world with insight and with vision. Today, we seek to more fully awaken this self within our Kingdom, that we might better discover our own responsibilities.

Our identity at **Yesod** is called *nefesh*, our animal soul, yet it has great possibilities. Only through the *nefesh* can we make sense out of the **Malchut** we meet. So we seek to honor that identity, and celebrate its energies in our world. This is the space in which we first open our "i's."

Daily Focus:

Within my world, I awaken now to a fuller appreciation of my individual being. I am filled with a new sense of my own integrity and uniqueness. I am more available than ever before to celebrate the One Being Who meets the world through me.

Meditation for the Forty-ninth Day

This is the final day of this journey. We began on the way out of enslavement. We walk now on the brink of Sinai, toward the Word which marks our awakening.

Today we focus our energies at **Malchut** in **Malchut**, the Grounding of the entire Tree of Life. We are here, in this world of countless wonders. This is where we must realize the energies of the Tree. This is the space in which and for which we have responsibility. The Light radiates at the base of the spine.

We are challenged to be true to ourselves and to our world, to perceive our own unfolding uniqueness and integrity in a world full of difficulties and confusions. We are called to discover the traces of all the *sefirot* which are hidden in this realm. We are the beings who can elevate the sparks which are hidden in this place, so that Creation may expand through the consciousness we carry.

It is not always easy to know our own uniqueness. There are so many voices which live within us and around us demanding that we conform to models fashioned by others.

How are we to know the way which is right for us at this moment? How are we to realize our own integrity? Perhaps by pausing long enough from our hectic lives to honor what we are actually thinking, feeling, and sensing. By knowing the "should's" and the "ought's," we are better able to meet ourselves and grow our own integrity. By daring to announce and accept ourselves as we are, we become available to our world and to ourselves. We already are the One we need to be.

Daily Focus:

I release the tensions that keep me from being fully present in my world. I become available to the inner whisper of direction as I accept myself and my world. I am ready to stand at the place of awakening called Sinai. I am ready to hear the Word that supports my World.

אדני

Open to the light of Shekinah — the dove of Pentecost — descending on the mountain top

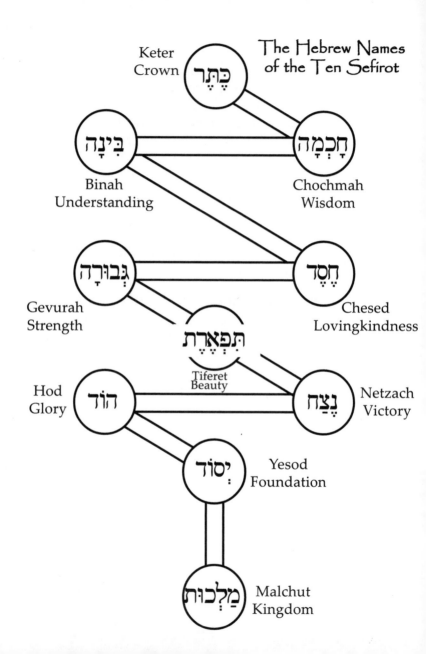

The Hebrew Names
of the Ten Sefirot

Keter
Crown — כֶּתֶר

Binah
Understanding — בִּינָה

Chochmah
Wisdom — חָכְמָה

Gevurah
Strength — גְּבוּרָה

Chesed
Lovingkindness — חֶסֶד

תִּפְאֶרֶת
Tiferet
Beauty

Hod
Glory — הוֹד

Netzach
Victory — נֶצַח

Yesod
Foundation — יְסוֹד

Malchut
Kingdom — מַלְכוּת

Growing Toward Completion

The completion of this Journey of Awareness brings a time of profound listening. This moment is symbolized by *Shavuot*, the Festival of Weeks, the celebration of the Revelation at Sinai. Energetically, we stand with our People at the foot of that ancient and always new Mountain. Again, we confront with awe the possibilities of that space.

In that ancient drama most of us remained below, afraid to approach the Mystery lest we be destroyed. We sent Moses up alone, that we might receive from him the Word. Perhaps now, at long last, we will face our fears when we meet at that Mountain of Revelation. Perhaps now, we will each become more available to receive that deep Teaching which is called Torah.

Revelation is unlike any other form of communication. All other forms of communication happen at a particular place and at a particular time. Revelation is communication outside the boundaries of normal space and time. Revelation is that communication which is always available to those who become receptive. That which was spoken is still being spoken. The Word at Sinai always awaits us, and each time it is received it is new.

Beginning with Blessing:

בָּרוּךְ אַתָּה יהוה אֱלֹהֵינוּ מֶלֶךְ הָעוֹלָם
שֶׁהֶחֱיָנוּ וְקִיְּמָנוּ וְהִגִּיעָנוּ לַזְּמַן הַזֶּה.

Baruch Atah Adonai Eloheynu Melech ha-olam, sheh-hehchiyanu, v'ki-y'manu, v'higi-anu laz'man hazeh.

Blessed are You, Eternal One our God, Universal Creative Presence, Who keeps us in life always, Who supports the unfolding of our uniqueness, and Who brings us to this very moment for blessing.

Though we stand as a Community at that Mountain, each of us must approach it on our own. There is but One message, translated through each of us according to our own levels of preparation, courage, and integrity. We can support each other with compassion, but the hearing is a responsibility that each must choose.

Meeting at the Mountain

After you have read the following guided meditative process, let your eyes close. Take some quiet time to enter into the scene on your own. Take advantage of this moment to discover this ancient/new place for yourself. Let it unfold for you. Become aware of the images that meet you, the impressions you receive. Perhaps there will be words, perhaps not. Then, gently, let your eyes open and record your experiences in your journal. Re-enter the scene as often as you like. Be available for that which awaits you there.

Trust the moment. The journey from enslavement to the freedom of awareness is real. Trust the images and the words you perceive. We are all awakening beings learning how to take greater responsibility for ourselves and for our world.

Let the following scene begin to take shape in your imagination.

A Guided Visualization

I stand at the foot of the Mountain now. There are others with me, and I experience a community of support. Each of us surrenders to our own awareness of this moment. I look up at the peak of that Mountain, aware of the Energy focused there. The Mountain almost pulsates with Light. There is a vibration which I begin to experience through every cell and every level of my being.

There is a path that calls to me now. I begin to walk. I become aware of the shifts in energy as I climb. The air feels fresher, more alive. The vibration grows so that I can hear it as a deep chanting sound within my mind. My steps grow lighter the higher I climb, almost as if some Force helps me up that incline.

I trust this place. I allow my awareness to be filled with the sights and sounds of the Mountain. And I discover a whisper of words, of images, of feelings that seem to rise from deep inside myself.

I take time now to enter into this scene. I find a place on the Mountain where I know I am to be still. I allow myself to listen. I am open to receive that which is mine to receive at this moment.

I am grateful for this holy opportunity.

Every Ending is a Beginning

The giving of Torah is an event which transcends our usual notions of time and space. The receiving of Torah is a process through which we awaken to the One we are. *Shavuot* celebrates the giving of Torah—the Torah which continually awaits our doing and our hearing. We are not only called upon to translate holy energies into words, we are called upon to translate the unfolding Torah into concrete action in the world. Through us, Torah lives. Through Torah, we find our truest Life.

Torah is not simply a document containing the first five books of the Hebrew Bible—Genesis, Exodus, Leviticus, Numbers and Deuteronomy—which speak to each generation with interpretations fresh and new. Torah is itself the Way called Judaism. It is the Heart of our faith, the Foundation of our tradition. It is the book with no end, supporting the expansion of our understandings of what it means to be a person, what it means to be a Jew, what it means to be a vehicle for the Spirit of Creation.

At holy moments, when we awaken to greater depths of our own being, we are receiving Torah. When we discover the meaning and purpose behind our existence, we are hearing that ancient Word in all its Life. There is no end to Torah. There is no end to the process of becoming witness to the Truth of our Being. There is no end to the exploration of the Being we share.

Shavuot is the symbol of that which cannot be contained in any particular calendar. The word *shavuot* literally means "weeks," and refers to the day after the seven-week journey from enslavement to Sinai is completed. The reality of *Shavuot* is with us always, and we celebrate it with special focus now. Our journey from self-imposed slavery to self-aware freedom is honored each and every time we open our "I's" to the fuller nature of our existence, to affirm our connection to All That Is, to celebrate our relationship to each other, to our world, and to The One we call our God.

Our meditative Journey has permitted us to retrace the steps of that path. Our Way challenges us to realize aspects of Universal Harmony that we might sing new songs of Creation. So this is a time to dream dreams, to recapture the Vision which has supported our trek through history, and to extend an unfolding Vision into what we think of as the future.

That Vision is perceived in the depths of our own souls. It is not hidden from us except by the accumulation of old patterns and old beliefs in our own limitations. It is we who erect the barriers to our own seeing; it is we who fill our consciousness with so much noise that we lose the gentle whisper of Oneness that is given to each of us in equal measure. So it is we who have the responsibility to step beyond those old habits and dare to receive that which we have not yet heard.

That there is always more of Torah for us to receive speaks the evolution of our faith and of ourselves. It is the basis of our seeking and the wonder of our finding. At its finest, our community supports the courage we each need to move beyond what we now know, to discover that which is about to be. In that discovery, and in the action it supports, new worlds are born.

So there is great promise in these moments. Our meditations are open-ended. They lead us to spaces in which we might hear and see and feel more deeply than ever before. Our meditations lead us into a space of trusting that we can know what we most need to know at any given moment. The truest Teacher awaits us within ourselves.

I release myself to the energies of my Mountain now. I stand at the summit and surrender to the Light which radiates around me. I see more clearly than ever before. I hear that which I have not yet heard. I realize the fuller wonder of my being.

I trust that these visions, these words, these realizations will expand within me for my greatest good and for the greatest good of all. Increasingly, I perceive that all the events of my life support my awakening.

I surrender to the holiness of this moment, and honor the Universal Presence Who blesses me all ways.

For Further Reading

Here are some suggestions for further study of the conceptual foundations of the meditations offered in this book, as well as further information about Judaism and Jewish meditation.

Kabbalah: The Way of the Jewish Mystic by Perle Epstein/ Perle Besserman (1978 Doubleday). An excellent basic introduction to the history and the dimensions of Kabbalah.

Meditation and Kabbalah by Aryeh Kaplan (1982 Samuel Weiser). A ground-breaking book translating and explaining selections from kabbalistic teachers through the ages. Kaplan provides a solid foundation for an understanding of Jewish meditative traditions.

Jewish Meditation: A Practical Guide by Aryeh Kaplan (1985 Schocken). Brief introductions and instructions in various Jewish meditative techniques.

God is a Verb: Kabbalah and the Practice of Mystical Judaism by Rabbi David Cooper (1997 Riverhead Books). David Cooper's books provide information and teaching encouraging deeper personal experiences of the Jewish meditative path.

Judaism For Dummies by Rabbi Ted Falcon, Ph.D. and David Blatner (2001 Hungry Minds). This is the first in the "For Dummies" series on religion to be published. Though I am hardly impartial, I think this is an excellent introduction not only to the whole of Jewish tradition, but to the mystical dimensions of Judaism as well.

Order Form

QTY.	Title	Price	Can. Price	Total
	A Journey of Awakening			
	Rabbi Ted Falcon, Ph.D.	$13.95	$17.95	
	Shipping and Handling			
	Add $3.50 for orders in the US			
	Sales tax (WA state residents only, add 8.9%			
	Total enclosed			

Telephone Orders:
Call 1-800-461-1931
Have your Visa or
MasterCard ready.

INTL. Telephone Orders:
Toll free 1-877-250-5500
Have your credit card ready.

Fax Order:
425-398-1380
Fill out this form and fax.

Postal Orders:
Hara Publishing
P.O. Box 19732
Seattle, WA 98109

E-mail Orders:
harapub@foxinternet.net

Method of Payment:

☐ Check or Money Order

☐ VISA

☐ MasterCard

_____
Card#

_____
Expiration Date

_____
Signature

Name_____

Address_____

City_____**State**_____**Zip**_____

Phone (   ) _____**Fax**_____

Quantity discounts are available.
Call 425-398-3679 for more information.
Thank you for your order!